Living the Life, One Pastor's Wife's Experiences

By Robin Smith

ISBN:
ISBN-13: 978-1721154371

DEDICATION

Dedication of this book goes to my husband, John, who asked me to live this life with him.

How beautiful on the mountains are the feet of those who bring good news, who proclaim peace, who bring good tidings, who proclaim salvation, who say to Zion, "Your God reigns!" – Isaiah 52:7 (NIV)

This book is also dedicated to my parents, Ken and Betty Sallee, who made sure I knew the Lord.

CONTENTS

Because I love those I will talk about and would not want to hurt anyone, I've changed everybody's names except for my husband's.

CHAPTER 1

ABOUT ME

As my grandfather said when I was about 3 months old and a tornado was going overhead, this girl is going to have an interesting life. I can't say it has been dull.

My birth indicates my life wasn't going to be normal. My parents lost twins the year before I was born. Grandma had come to help my mom. As she sat in the small-town hospital waiting room, she heard something snap. All she could think was that they had lost me as well. Then she heard me scream from the pain of breaking my right arm during birth!

To top off the day, I was born during the worst blizzard to hit western Kansas in 50 years. The weather was so bad when my dad returned home from the hospital he found the front door glass had been broken by the high winds of the blizzard and the snow had blown into the little house. He had to dig his way into the house. The phone was ringing and ringing (for those of you who are too young to know this, they didn't have answering machines or voice mail back then.) As he got to the phone, the highway patrol stopped by to check on him. It had been Mom and Grandma calling to check if he made it home okay. Someone at the hospital called her husband, who was a patrolman, and asked him to check on Dad.

Growing Up In Church

My dad hadn't grown up attending church and it wasn't until he and Mom were dating that he was introduced to the Lord. He became a Christian before they got married. Now my dad was determined his children would be going to church.

Growing up, I was in church every Sunday unless I was sick. Absolutely no skipping allowed. Like any other kid, I tried to pretend to be sick. Dad said I needed to prove I was sick. You know what that meant, throwing up or a temperature. Foiled! The one thing I can say is the Lord is so right – **"Train up a child in the way he should go, and when he is old he will not depart from it."** - Proverbs 22:6. I can't even think of skipping church.

Vacations And Church

When it came to vacations, there wasn't a vacation from church. On Saturdays, my dad would scope out a church for us to attend on Sunday morning. By the end of our vacation we would have a bulletin from each church we attended.

You might wonder why we took our bulletins home. We were rewarded for our Sunday school attendance. Over the years I have lost my church attendance pins, but each of us kids had them.

My world revolved around our church life. We

spent many hours with families from church - from camping, picnics, parties, cookouts and having each other over for homemade ice cream and cake on Sunday evenings. The fathers played ball on Friday nights. My babysitting business was kids from church. A bond was built with our church family.

While I was in high school, we moved and the local church wasn't at all like what we had before. Unfortunately, during this time, our whole family stopped attending church. Truth be told, this drove me nuts, but I was too shy to attend church by myself.

I Feel A Change Coming

For the Spirit God gave us does not make us timid, but gives us power, love and self-discipline. – 2 Timothy 1:7 (NIV)

I got a job in Oklahoma. I wanted to be back in church but my shyness kept me out. Occasionally, I would be able to convince my aunt to visit a church with me. But I just couldn't go to church by myself. The Lord sent three ladies from a church I had visited a year earlier. It turned out one of the ladies was my future best friend, Judy.

The Lord placed me with a group of Christians who were quickly growing spiritually. I believe he was equipping me for the position that lay ahead of me. At this time, I had major drama going on that wasn't of my doing. Because I had the Lord and my Sunday School Class, I didn't fear for my life. The Lord was my Shield and Comforter for sure during this time.

One Sunday, as I was sitting in church, the associate

pastor's wife gave her testimony. She told how she was able to witness to this group or that person. As a very shy person, I decided it would be easier to witness if I were married to a minister. So, I prayed for the position! *Be careful what you pray for*.

How God Works And Suspicious Minds

After a year with this wonderful group and the tremendous spiritual growth, the church leadership decided to separate us by age. (In doing this, many in the class, including myself, left to other churches.) I attended several other churches, on my own. Yes, on my own; see how the Lord works!

A couple of ladies I worked with invited me to attend their church. I did, and I loved the church and the people there. Eventually, I would meet my future husband there.

The only thing that was hard to get past was that some women at this church thought I was there to steal their husbands. Not this girl!

Now I'm not an athlete in any shape or form, but I joined the ladies' softball team. To my horror I found out most of the ladies were into fast pitch. Being left-handed, I was to play one of two positions: outfield or first base. This was terrifying, as I can't catch or hit a ball.

We had practice just before the first game. As I stood there in the outfield, one woman went to bat and she hit that ball hard. It flew my direction. To my amazement I caught the ball, but it kept going right into my shin. I had a goose egg on my leg and could barely walk.

I went with the team to the ball diamond and praised the Lord I couldn't play. This ball diamond wasn't flat. The outfield sloped down to a pond. I knew if I were playing, every ball coming my way would've ended up in the pond. Our ladies were so good that our games ended in the second inning. They didn't allow a huge score difference. We placed first in the finals. I actually got a plaque for it! Yes, the girl on the bench got a plaque!

It was a couple years later before the Lord brought John into my life. In the meantime, my aunt kept telling me I needed to go to a church where there would be better prospects for finding a husband. I asked her, "What if I was in the wrong place when God sent the man he wanted me to marry?" Just because I was at a church where I was the only single person, doesn't mean God won't answer my prayer.

John and two other ministerial students, Jacob and Charles, came to the church I was attending. Finally, I wasn't the only single person at church.

After the morning service one Sunday, Louise, one of the ladies who invited me to attend this church, asked me to come for lunch with the college and high school students.

John impressed me during this lunch. Jacob and Charles were fighting over a high school girl who was TROUBLE. As the two young men verbally fought over her, I watched her glow with delight.

...correction and instruction are the way to life, keeping you from your neighbor's wife, from the smooth talk of a wayward woman. Do not lust in your heart after her beauty or let her captivate you with her eyes. – Proverbs 6:23b-25 (NIV)

After returning to church for the evening service, I saw John stop Jacob as he was coming down a staircase. Jacob was very short. John and Jacob were now at eye level. John had one hand on Jacob's shoulder and he was shaking his finger in front of Jacob's face. John was rebuking Jacob for not displaying Christ-like behavior. John's lecture got Jacob back to acting more like a Christian should. Charles would be rebuked later, away from the church, as he was the winner of the fight and was with Carol.

Easter came, and by this time, people noticed that John had taken a liking to me. His attention was always on me.

Several weeks after Easter, my parents came to visit my grandmother, who lived about two hours away. I decided it was a good time to see everyone.

While I was there, John received a call that his dad was diagnosed with black lung cancer. The college immediately sent him home to Kentucky. Within two months John's dad had died. The only news I had was through friends in college and they hadn't heard anything since his dad had passed away.

The fall came and went, and John hadn't returned, and there was no news from him. That Christmas was a time of tears for me. Not meaning to hurt me, my sister-in-law asked me why I wasn't married and when I would be. It wasn't like I was the one in control of the situation. That night I cried and talked with my mother. We sat there and prayed. I was so lonely and wanted a husband, even if it was John. Yes, I said EVEN John! There wasn't anything wrong with him, except that he was seven years younger than me, which was my hang-up.

The Phone Rang

When I got home from work one Wednesday night in January, I found a note on my apartment door saying they were spraying for bugs on Thursday. Lovely! This meant a very busy evening for me. I had to empty all the cabinets, or they wouldn't spray. No mid-week service for this girl. I had to stay home from church.

Shortly after church was over, the phone rang. It was Louise. "Robin, guess who was at church tonight? And, guess who was looking for you?" It didn't take long for me to guess it was John. Mentally, I had put on my running shoes.

The Bible College John and his friends were attending didn't serve any meals on Sundays, so our ladies were taking turns inviting them to their homes for Sunday lunch. I was on the list to feed them.

When my Sunday came, the guys asked what I was going to serve them before they would even agree to come. I informed them I had spaghetti. Immediately, they were eager to come to my place. It turned out everyone had been feeding them fried chicken on Sundays.

John finally asked me for a date. He planned to come over and make me lunch on Saturday. His omelet turned into scrambled eggs. Over the years, he has improved his omelet-making abilities tremendously. In fact, it has become our tradition for John to make omelets and serve me breakfast in bed on our anniversary every year.

We started seeing each other and our dates consisted of discussing our beliefs. The first few dates were all very serious talks with 11 hours of discussion. We never left my dining room table, or I was on the sofa and he was in my wingback chair. I knew John shouldn't marry a woman who could destroy his ministry by going behind him and disagreeing with his preaching and teaching.

John had been called into the ministry at age 16, the time of his salvation. Needless to say, I knew what I was getting into if we got married. This doesn't mean I was ready to hop right into the position as a pastor's wife.

My parents had told me of their pastor's wife standing up in the service and telling her husband he was wrong as he preached. This had put a bad taste in their mouths towards her and it weighed heavy on my mind.

A woman can make or break her husband. I'd hate to stand in front of the Lord and answer for destroying the ministry of God's man.

While we were dating, I got a call one Wednesday from the State Office wanting me to be the secretary for the second-in-command. I was to give my answer on Friday, but I kept getting calls all afternoon, asking if I had an answer. If I had applied for the position it would have been one thing, but this was out of the blue.

This job meant moving an hour away. I had renewed my lease and, at that time, getting a job in another city wasn't an excuse to break a contract. Then there was John to think about. I was so torn. The pay would be great and I would be able to get promotions. But I didn't know what to do.

I went to church that night and asked for prayer. Since John worked cleaning offices he wasn't able to attend Wednesday night services.

When John got back on campus, Jacob met him. He didn't tell John what was going on, other than "Robin needs you to call her NOW". It was about 11:30 that night when I got the phone call from John. We talked and prayed for an hour. During our discussion and after praying, John had me say "I'll take the job" and then had me say "I won't take the job." After each statement, I was to tell him how I felt. I was uneasy after "I'll take the job" and at ease with "I won't take the job."

John told me I should take Thursday off because of the calls. While I was off, I still prayed for the Lord's will. First thing Friday morning, as you can guess, I got a call. I told them no thank you. I had total peace!

Marriage Proposals

John told me he was going to marry me at the end of our first date. I informed him I had been hurt before and had a large wall around me. To which he replied he and the Lord would break down that wall.

From that day on, John proposed every day. Sometimes, I was asked more than once a day. I kept telling him the Lord was trying to teach him patience, which he hadn't learned. It took four months before I finally said, "Okay."

We've been married 30 years and he has pastored the same amount of time. He is my best friend, soul mate, husband, and **my pastor**.

CHAPTER 2
AUNT RUBY

But be sure to fear the Lord and serve him faithfully with all your heart; consider what great things he has done for you. - 1 Samuel 12:24 (NIV)

Once I was engaged, my mother contacted her Aunt Ruby. She had been a pastor's wife most of her life. My mom wanted her to give me advice.

Praise the Lord pastors aren't paid like they were in the past. Aunt Ruby and her husband had been paid by members bringing food. Relying on what was given could really bring hardship. She had seen it all.

I had heard stories from an aunt who had visited Aunt Ruby and found a life she wouldn't want. Examples are: deacon's kids showing up Sunday morning expecting Aunt Ruby to get them ready for church; or, with very little food, deacons showing up at lunch thinking they should be fed.

Aunt Ruby wrote to me but informed me she wouldn't give me advice except what is listed below. If you notice, this advice goes for everyone, not just pastors and their wives, except for number five which applies only to Pastors and their wives.

1. Do not worry if your husband only has one suit: he can only wear one at a time.
2. Do not to talk about church problems in front of your children. They don't need to be taking sides against friends because of church issues.
3. When brought into the middle of a disagreement, be careful as to taking sides. The person who is right might be exhibiting an ungodly attitude. You don't want to be seen agreeing with an ungodly attitude.
4. Understand you cannot have close friends within the members of the church. You can't share everything with members as it can come back to hurt you, your husband, family, and/or the church.
5. The first people who welcome you to the pastorate with open arms will be the first to be ready for you to leave.

Number four has been the hardest for me. I haven't had the privilege of living close enough to family that I can pop over, but when I've lived closer to family, the road only goes one way.

"You have said, 'It is futile to serve God. What do we gain by carrying out his requirements and going about like mourners before the Lord Almighty? But now we call the arrogant blessed. Certainly evildoers prosper, and even

when they put God to the test, they get away with it.'" Then those who feared the Lord talked with each other, and the Lord listened and heard. A scroll of remembrance was written in his presence concerning those who feared the Lord and honored his name. "On the day when I act," says the Lord Almighty, "they will be my treasured possession. I will spare them, just as a father has compassion and spares his son who serves him. And you will again see the distinction between the righteous and the wicked, between those who serve God and those who do not. – Malachi 3:14-18 (NIV)

CHAPTER 3

LONELINESS

Bless those who persecute you; bless and do not curse. Rejoice with those who rejoice; mourn with those who mourn. Live in harmony with one another. Do not be proud but be willing to associate with people of low position. Do not be conceited. Do not repay anyone evil for evil. Be careful to do what is right in the eyes of everybody. If it is possible, as far as it depends on you, live at peace with everyone. Do not take revenge, my friends, but leave room for God's wrath, for it is written: "It is mine to avenge; I will repay," says the Lord. On the contrary: "If your enemy is hungry, feed him; if he is thirsty, give him something to drink. In doing this, you will heap burning coals on his head." Do not be overcome by evil, but overcome evil with good. – Romans 12:14-21 (NIV)

As a pastor's wife, I've found times that the only ones I can lean on are the Lord and my husband. Since this isn't the happiest of topics, I want to get it over with at the beginning. There are plenty of "oh my", "you've got to be kidding", and, outright giggles remaining in this book.

I understood, but at the same time I didn't. You shouldn't confide in church members.

A lot has to do with spiritual maturity. I am in no way saying the Lord made the pastor or his wife more spiritually mature because of their position. It has to do with those who are around you. If you lay out your concerns to other church members, will they become burdened in prayer, or, be someone to spread what you said around the church or town?

Then, there is the fact, especially in small towns, that you are an outsider. Everyone already had their quota of friends before you came. They have their friends who they grew up with and their extended family.

Over the years, I have experienced some of what Christ experienced in the garden. You know, where our Lord takes a few disciples to pray with Him. He goes and pours His heart out to the Heavenly Father and returns to find the disciples are sleeping. How often do we sleep instead of praying for and with our pastor's wife and our brothers and sisters in Christ? When you are praying with someone, you are standing with them. The Lord wanted the presence of man, how much more do we need the presence of each other and the Lord?

Recently, I was watching the movie *Mom's Night Out*, and the pastor's wife thanks the ladies for inviting her out with them. She tells them she hasn't been invited out with the ladies in five years. I realized when she made that statement I had tears running down my cheeks. Oh, how I could relate!

When my husband has been very ill, rarely have I had someone in the church console me. They might ask how he was doing, but more for information to judge him, than out of concern. Rarely have I heard, "how are you doing?" or "Robin, I love you".

It's at these times I've never felt more alone. I've sat in the pew with tears streaming down my face while someone filled in at the pulpit. Only the Lord and the one preaching knew the pain I was going through, as they could see my tears.

Please understand that I'm not blaming the ladies of the church; just be aware that the one person hurting most in the church could be the pastor's wife.

John calls me Pollyanna. For those of you who don't know, Pollyanna looked for the good in every situation. When you don't see Pollyanna in me, know I'm hurting. At these times I want to stand up and yell "People, can't you see I'm hurting?" But I can't. I'm not trying to mask my feelings, as that would be a lie, but at the same time I don't want to say the wrong thing. I am very sure other pastors' wives have felt the same.

I'm just trying to hold myself together. If I let everyone know how I feel, I can visualize the men hurrying out because they don't know how to respond to female emotions. I can't say how women would respond. I hope they would hug me and pray with me. But I'm not going to disturb the church service. The focus of the service should be on the Lord.

CHAPTER 4

LOOKING FOR A CHURCH

The Trying Out Begins

The end of all things is near. Therefore be clear minded and self-controlled so that you can pray. Above all, love each other deeply because love covers a multitude of sins. Offer hospitality to one another without grumbling.- 1 Peter 4:7-9 (NIV)

Trying out for a church is one of the most nerve-wracking times for me. We belong to one of the few denominations which use this method to select a new pastor. I don't mind just going to preach at a church. But feeling like you're doing tryouts for a play or musical is just hard on me.

Before John got his first pastorate, we went to several churches "to try out". Driving halfway across the state on Sunday morning for a tryout, we arrived at a beautiful church. If John hadn't been given directions to the church it would have been hard to find since there was no GPS in those days.

A new church stood in the middle of a field down a gravel road. It looked like they had just graveled the parking lot because there were no ruts from the cars.

We got there before Sunday school. The parking lot and the church were packed. We were thrilled to see a full church for Sunday school. As John greeted people, he asked the church leaders about the outreach of the church since the church was so full. This turned out to be the wrong question. Seems this church was built for "me, mine, and no more."

After the morning service, we were invited over to a member's house for lunch. This had already been planned before we came. I don't think we would've been asked if they realized we were interested in more church growth. Since we would be staying for the evening service, John asked if he could take a nap as he had worked all night at OU doing night watch. He had gotten off work with enough time to come home, change clothes, and get on the road.

This became an afternoon of misery for me. The host family didn't want to have anything to do with me. They sat in one area of the room and I sat where I had been seated after lunch. The family talked among themselves and did not include me in any of the conversations. I could hardly wait for that day to end so that we could head home.

We heard by midweek that they weren't interested in us. No surprise!

Then John was asked to tryout at a church not far

from where we lived. The candidate who had tried out the week before showed up. This made things very awkward in the lobby after the service.

The situation only got worse when the wife of one of the pulpit committee members announced there was no way she was having us come over for lunch. You could've heard a pin drop after she did this. We hadn't planned on eating with anyone.

Again, we got a phone call saying the church decided they would go with the candidate who showed up while we were there.

Another church asked John to come tryout. John had been there before as it was another young preacher's home church. It was close by. I don't remember much about the service, only that after the church service I had to walk through a cloud of cigarette smoke to get to our car. No, it wasn't the men of the church who lit up, but the ladies. There wasn't a single lady not smoking.

The Call

He said to them, "Go into all the world
and preach the gospel to all creation. –
Mark 6:15 (NIV)

John got a call from a deacon begging him to tryout at his church. It seemed nobody wanted this church. They couldn't even get someone to fill-in while they were without a pastor.

John finally gave in. We had discussed over and over that we weren't going to take this church. If they wanted John to preach until they found someone else, we might do it.

When we got there, we found a little cinder block church with an old single wide trailer as their parsonage.

After the Sunday evening service, I went into the restroom to change into comfortable clothing as we had a 3-hour drive to get home. While changing I started laughing. I couldn't stop. John could hear me in the lobby.

Remember, we had decided on the way there, we were not going to take this church no matter what. Once we got in the car to leave, John asked me what I was laughing about in the ladies' room. I informed him this was the church he was to pastor. John grinned as God had told him the same. We had said no to each other and to the Lord, but that wasn't what God had planned.

CHAPTER 5

THE LIFE BEGINS

Parsonage Life

Jesus replied, "Foxes have holes, and birds of the air have nests, but the Son of Man has no place to lay His head."
– Matthew 8:20 (NIV)

During our engagement, John had explained to me some of what might happen in a pastor's home; especially, the worst possible scenario. John knew a pastor who had a deacon unlock the door to the parsonage and go in while only the pastor's wife was home. The pastor's wife came out of the shower to find the man standing in the living room. That afternoon the pastor changed the locks. I can say I haven't had anyone unlock my door and come in unannounced. Some church members believe they can have access to the parsonage without asking if they can enter.

John said parsonage life could be difficult. He said he believed it would be better to live in a single wide semi-trailer. That way we could just move the trailer, making it easier when changing churches.

I was given other parsonage advice from the most unlikely people before we got married. My boss, at the time of our marriage, was one. He didn't attend church. I knew he had in the past but was stunned to find out he had been a church elder. He told me he had to talk to me about being a pastor's wife. The church in which he had served as an elder supplied a furnished parsonage.

I remember smiling at him and telling him he knew I had my own furniture. Jim informed me that didn't matter, what I needed to understand was the mindset of the church members. They wouldn't necessarily believe in taking care of the parsonage and the pastor.

He then went on to tell me what had happened while he was on the elder board. The pastor approached the board and asked if the board would supply his family with a new sofa. When they moved in, the sofa had legs missing and those remaining weren't good. His family had been using books to keep the sofa up. After listening to the pastor's plea, one of the men on the board said he had an old sofa in the barn. It would do fine after he cleaned it up some.

I know each of you can picture that sofa sitting in the loft of the barn. It is covered with hay. Who knows what animal/rodent has been on it. Good enough for the animals in the barn, good enough for the pastor.

Thus, the parsonage had a new sofa fresh from the barn!

Jim went on to tell me another time the pastor informed them the garbage disposal had broken, again. Another member said," my wife wants a new disposal, I'll get her a new one and you can have the old one."

His final illustration was how the members of this church had gotten very upset when the pastor's father died and left him money. The pastor was able to get his own home and furniture.

Blessing Or Headache

But Ruth replied, "... Where you go I will go, and where you stay I will stay. Your people will be my people and your God my God. – Ruth 1:16 (NIV)

So, at $75 a week, a parsonage and paid utilities, we moved to our first church. As you can guess, John had to be bi-vocational, but the Lord provided him a job at a computer store.

Very few churches supply pastors with parsonages these days. So, chances now of having a parsonage like this are slim, or the pastor says, "No way."

My family helped us move in. As we walked into the trailer everyone made a noise of astonishment. My sister-in-law took one look at the ceiling hanging down and said, "You must truly be 'called'. There isn't any way I'd live here." My 6'4" brother had to stoop over while walking in the living room so he wouldn't hit his head on the ceiling which bowed that low. Parsonage living can help you financially but can also be a headache.

I need to explain so you will understand the layout of the trailer. At the west end was the master bedroom. In the master bedroom there was enough room for a bed; the closet was on the north side of the room and had the hot water tank in it; and the dryer hookup was also in the room on the east wall.

On the other side of the wall was the bathroom, which had the washer hookup. Then there was a small bedroom; and the next room was the kitchen. The living room and another bedroom were past the kitchen.

It wouldn't take much wind to move the walls of the trailer. You could watch the paneling and the siding move and see outside when the wind blew.

When we were asked to pastor the church, we were informed we would never have the pipes freeze, as they had wrapped them. Even though I had been told this, I left water dripping during a blizzard. Guess what? You've got it; even then, the pipes froze.

John was unable to help me get the pipes thawed because he had caught the mumps at work. The school system was highly infected but teachers were coming to get software from the computer store. The congregation wouldn't help because John was sick, even though they had already had the mumps. I was the one who, to this day, hasn't had them.

Finally, we had a day when John's swelling had gone down. We decided we had to get the laundry done. So, we took all of our laundry to the local laundry mat. I loaded five washers and washed everything I had. As I was loading the wet laundry up to take back to the trailer, John wondered if I wanted to dry the clothes there. I said "No, we have a perfectly good dryer in the trailer."

We went back to the trailer and I proceeded to put the clothing into the dryer. Remember, this is in the master bedroom where the hot water tank was located, and the cold north wind had frozen the hot water tank.

After running a load or two in our dryer, the pipes thawed out! The bathroom sink was on the other side of the wall from the dryer. I haven't a clue what happened, but as the water began to thaw, water came up out of the sink's drain. Yes, from the drain, and water was shooting towards the ceiling like a fountain. It was going everywhere.

I ran to the phone and called men of the church. Almost immediately, the excitement really began. The water meter was in front of the church, out of the view of the trailer. Lucas came and turned off the water at the meter and proceeded to come into the trailer.

Then Howard came and turned the water back on, not knowing somebody had already turned it off. I felt like I was living in a Keystone Cop movie. This happened several times and the water was going everywhere. It was moving like "The Blob" from room to room. Eventually, the water had gone from the bathroom, to the spare bedroom, into the kitchen, and was approaching the living room.

We had a Boston bull terrier, Shadrach. He had the habit of turning his head away from you as you scolded him; occasionally he would look at you from the corners of his big eyes during the scolding.

That night, as the water crept towards the living room, Shadrach sat on the sofa staring straight ahead towards the front door. Occasionally, he'd look out of the corners of his eyes as the water approached the sofa. We had to laugh as we knew he was telling us "No way is that my puddle."

I'll Fly Away

The stove was electric. I love the retro look and this stove looked a lot like old stoves. It had six burners, a door to the left of the oven for cooking sheets, and a drawer below for pots and pans. The burners occasionally made noise while I was cooking. At one point, one burner arced to the ceiling and left a burnt spot on the ceiling.

We told the church, but the church wasn't in any hurry to get it fixed. For weeks, I cooked our meals in an electric skillet. When the repairman came, we found out the previous stove had been gas and wasn't properly closed off. We could have gone "BOOM" at any time! When the repairman found the issue, I, along with a little boy I was watching, was sent to the street in case the house blew up during the repair. Praise the Lord, nothing happened.

Watching You

As a pastor and wife, you will find people are always watching you. Your home life is judged. A church member, who lived two doors down from us, watched our every move. The previous pastor told us he and his wife were sure this woman could tell you how many times you went to the bathroom!

At another parsonage, John had the habit of sitting on the front porch reading his Bible and drinking coffee. People from other churches would stop and let him know they felt the world was okay when they saw him there.

A Flag?

You, my brothers and sisters, were called to be free. But do not use your freedom to indulge the flesh; rather, serve one another humbly in love. – Galatians 5:13 (NIV)

John was licensed to preach but hadn't been ordained yet. Finally, we were able to have a service. Working it into the calendar of other pastors as well as ours made it land on April 16. Since April 15th fell on Saturday that year, taxes weren't due until Monday, April 17 that year. My brother, a CPA, dropped his busy schedule to be at the service. Other family members also came to attend this service.

My nieces sat on the front row. John had asked Ben, a preacher in our area to do the sermon at the service. Brother Ben was from Tennessee, so he had a deep accent and preached very loudly. Watching my nieces and my cousin's daughters as this man preached got me tickled. Each time he got louder, their eyes got bigger and their necks stretched back as if this would put them in the pew behind them.

After the service was over, we had a few family members come over to the trailer to celebrate. My aunts had questions. Brother Ben had my family lost in the sermon. "Why was it so bad to pick up a flag?" I sat there a few minutes trying to remember a "flag" in the sermon. Then it dawned on me that the word they had misunderstood was, "plague". Then they understood.

"Many people thought being called into the ministry as picking up the plague."

Cooking With Lard

I know this is a thing of the past now, but our ladies cooked with lard. We were told we were living in the widow capital of the United States. It didn't take long for John and me to figure out why. The bucket was on the back porch.

I'm not saying their cooking was terrible. Oh, they could cook! The ladies at our church cooked once a week for the Lions Club and then once a month for the Chamber of Commerce. If it hadn't been for these hardworking ladies, the church wouldn't have the fellowship hall.

I know I probably had my mouth open in shock as they were cooking. They would put a cup of oil in the green beans! And, when they made a cake, another cup of oil was poured in the bottom of a cake pan before pouring in the cake batter! My stomach hurt from all the oil and lard they used.

Our ladies even supplied cookies for the bank's open house at Christmas. The Lions Club had a chili supper once a year and we supplied the pies. They were making money hand over fist, as the expression goes.

In our congregation, we only had four men, including my husband. One man was single and the rest had wives. Ninety-five percent of our ladies were widows. Loved with lard!

Mohawk

When John took the pastorate, the church had a deacon who had married his first cousin, just as his dad had done. Unfortunately, the family had problems because of intermarrying. Their son only came to church once, when he was out of prison. This young man had so many problems.

His sisters had proudly told us their brother had given himself a mohawk by pulling his hair out of his head. Yes, pulled it out!

They warned John he was also a pyromaniac. That Sunday afternoon, this young man shows up at the trailer door wanting to talk with John. They went over to the church. I sat at home praying and praying. I was so scared for John's safety. I couldn't call to check on him as the house and church phone were one and the same.

You say, "Why wouldn't you go over to the church and check on John?" Makes sense, right? It would if I hadn't already been instructed, when we were dating, not to do so.

This lesson was learned because the pastor's wife at the church where we were married had interrupted her husband while he was counseling someone in his office. John and I witnessed this. She burst in the door and told him it was time for him to go home as it was past his bedtime. At that moment, I was told I was never to interrupt John while counseling.

After what seemed an eternity, John returned to the trailer. Praise the Lord the young man didn't harm anyone or anything.

Tattoos

For the wages of sin is death, but the

gift of God is eternal life in Christ Jesus our Lord. – Romans 6:23 (NIV)

Every church is a mission. Upon arriving at church one Wednesday night, I was given a fright. A man on a motorcycle pulled up and got off. He had long scraggly hair and you could see that he had tattoos from his chin down; even his fingers had tattoos.

It was just the two of us there at the church. I had gotten there before John, so the church was still locked and I wasn't going to be alone with this man in an empty building.

Max looked at me and asked me if Joseph was here. It should have been obvious that there was nobody else there but us. I informed him Joseph had not yet arrived.

It wasn't long until someone from church showed up and I felt comfortable enough to unlock the doors of the church.

This man, Max, had met Joseph at counseling for those who had been in prison. Max had just gotten out of prison after serving 16 years for stabbing his girlfriend to death! And Joseph invited him to church.

I think the man thought coming to church was just a way to have fun by ridiculing Christians because he kept bringing prostitutes to church. He would sit on the back pew trying to disturb the worship service. This went on for over a year.

I remember being asked at work how things were going at church. I said we had a murderer and prostitutes coming to church. The person looked at me and stated they didn't know we were a mission church. Excuse me, but all Bible believing and teaching churches are mission churches!

During this time, he and one of the prostitutes had a baby girl. Because of Max's baby girl, he tried to straighten out his life. But he and the prostitute got into it about the baby and he ended up in a halfway house.

While Max was in the halfway house, he called John and asked John to come see him. Since Max had never respected John at all John was rather nervous. I told him I'd be praying for him. John was gone for hours.

When John came home I ask him how things went. John, still rather stunned, told me how the Lord had worked. When John entered the halfway house, Max was on the other side of the room. Upon seeing John come in, Max ran at him. John said he didn't know what to expect, but Max grabbed John up in his arms and hugged him. He wanted to accept the Lord as his Savior and wanted to talk to John about his daughter.

I wish I could say he lived happily ever after, but probably less than six months later, Max died in a car crash.

Nevertheless, God's solid foundation stands firm, sealed with this inscription: "The Lord knows those who are his," and, "Everyone who confesses the name of the Lord must turn away from wickedness." - 2 Timothy 2:19 (NIV)

Roaring Lion

Be self-controlled and alert. Your enemy the devil prowls around like a

roaring lion looking for someone to devour. Resist him, standing firm in the faith, because you know that your brothers throughout the world are undergoing the same kind of sufferings. And the God of all grace, who called you to His eternal glory in Christ, after you have suffered a little while, will Himself restore you and make you strong, firm and steadfast.
– 1 Peter 5:8-10 (NIV)

The church had a custom of reviewing the pastor after the first three months. Things had been going so well and they forgot the review except for one man. He decided to ask each member only one question, "Has the pastor or his wife ever offended you?"

We were totally unaware this was taking place. Another member told John what was being held against us. I watched my husband cry over his charges:

- Not preaching loud enough for those sitting on the back row, who need hearing aids, to hear;
- Inviting people outside the church to attend;
- Doing too much visitation;
- I hadn't invited someone into the house while I was sick; and the best,
- Not sending flowers to a family when their mother died two months before we even knew the church existed.

Right now, I need to say something about bringing charges against God's messengers, whether a minister, Sunday school teacher, deacon, etc. Be very careful. If you destroy a ministry the Lord has ordained, know you will be held accountable for doing so. There are people within the church who think it is their God-given position to keep people humble. They tie the hands or tongue of the messenger. I have witnessed many a young man called to preach, who the congregation destroyed, never to minister again.

I remember my parents surprised us by dropping by on their way home from my brother's that night. My dad looked at John and told him to wipe the dust from his feet.

If people do not welcome you, leave their town and shake the dust off your feet as a testimony against them." – Luke 9:5 (NIV)

Once the people figured out we had learned about the phone calls and the results, they got mad at each other. They couldn't bear the sight of each other. So, the number of people attending church dropped. In fact, there were Sundays when there were only four of us in attendance. Ed was one of those John had invited to come to church. He came every week. You can do the numbers: John, Ed, me, and a different person each week.

John invited another minister to preach one Sunday. The members came to hear him. After the service, that minister told John he had a church John needed to pastor. When he returned home, he contacted the church and they called asking us to tryout.

We went the next Sunday morning. John preached both Sunday morning and evening. That night this church voted 100% to have John come as their pastor. John told them we would take the position.

Back at John's current pastorate, the news got out John had tried out at another church. So, Wednesday night EVERYONE showed up. I felt like I was in a Frankenstein movie. They were mad that we would even think about leaving!

John informed me before the service started that I wasn't to say a word. He would take all heated words. It was so hard to listen to the things being said to John.

Ed stood up and rebuked them. He asked them where they had been. He went on to say John had every right to kick the dust off his feet. This man brought them down; the room was quiet.

That servant who knows his master's will and does not get ready and does not do what his master wants will be beaten with many blows. But the one who does not know and does things deserving punishment will be beaten with few blows. From everyone who has been given much, much will be demanded, and from the one who has been entrusted with much, much more will be asked. - Luke 12:47 & 48 (NIV)

A New Beginning

We moved to the new community and church. This church also supplied us with a parsonage. We enjoyed having a roomy parsonage. The previous pastor had been a cabinet maker, so the kitchen had been redone. The carpet in the house had come out of members' homes when they put new carpet in their homes. This meant cigarette burns in the carpet. The plumbing regularly needed to be cleared because the neighbor's line ran into ours.

Since the parsonage was larger, I felt I could entertain. So, I invited the deacon Dick, and his wife Anne, over for supper one evening. Upon entering the house, Anne informed me with a manner of disgust, "No pastor and his wife have *EVER* arranged the furniture this way!"

"Okay," I thought.

We started to eat supper. I had made my most requested items for church dinners - BBQ meatballs, cheesy potatoes, salad and a dessert. Again, Anne insulted me, "I could have made this meal better!"

I know other pastor's wives might have cried upon her leaving the house, but Praise the Lord, my parents had made me be in 4-H from the age of seven into high school. Growing up, many tears had fallen while making items for the fairs. Knowing I had gone to the State Fair more than once with my cooking, made her words roll off my back. I was able to laugh quietly in my heart and go on. Believe it or not, Anne and I became friends.

Tithes And Missions

Will a man rob God? Yet you rob me. But you ask, "How do we rob you?" In tithes and offerings. You are under a curse – the whole nation of you – because you are robbing me. Bring in the whole tithe into the storehouse, that there may be food in my house. Test me in this, says the Lord Almighty, and see if I will not throw open the floodgates of heaven and pour out so much blessing that you will not have room enough for it. – Malachi 3:8-10 (NIV)

I have sat in more than one church service where a husband and wife discussed, as the offering plate came by, which tithe check to put in, this week's check or the one they made out last week and didn't put in as they hadn't come to church. I wanted to lean towards them and yell BOTH!

Do not take a purse or bag or sandals; and do not greet anyone on the road. When you enter a house, first say, 'Peace to this house.' If someone who promotes peace is there, your peace will rest on them; if not, it will return to you. Stay there, eating and drinking whatever they give you, for the worker deserves his wages. Do not move around from house to house. – Luke 10:4-7 (NIV

Now our church believed in tithing and missions, but others in our area didn't. A preacher of our denomination had come through the area in the 1920's to 1940's and started churches or did revivals. He didn't believe at the time in tithing and missions. The people in this area grabbed onto this teaching and wouldn't let go of it. As a side note, this preacher later came to understand that tithing and missions were scriptural; but the damage was done, and people wouldn't give up even though they saw it in scripture.

We hadn't lived in the area very long when another church of our denomination was having a revival. Some of our church members decided they wanted to attend. John drove the church van to take those who wished to attend. The church having the revival was one that didn't believe in tithing and missions. John went in and sat down. Before the service started, some of those who didn't believe in tithing and missions came and told him he should leave. They didn't say anything to our members, just John. John didn't leave. As time went by, John was known for standing his ground.

Fundraising

Now I have said our church believed in tithing and missions, but the truth is the Ladies Auxiliary did. We had those men who saw it but didn't believe it.

John decided he wanted the church to give a large offering for missions on Easter. His plan was to get the kids of the church involved. The month before Easter, John went to the kids' Sunday school classes and asked the kids to collect pennies. The kids took the challenge. When the kids approached the adults, the adults informed the kids they wanted to collect their own change for the offering.

John had told the kids they would bring their offering up to the offertory table during the service. John decided he wouldn't change this. When Easter Sunday came, trusting the Lord to multiply, we brought out the punch bowl and put it on the offertory table. I stood beside the pianist and sang as the people came up row by row and placed their money in the punch bowl. The pianist, Bernice, sat there laughing and crying as people who didn't believe in tithing were putting money in the bowl. It took three of us to carry the punch bowl out of the sanctuary! We had collected over $250 in change.

Don't we have the right to food and drink? Don't we have the right to take a believing wife along with us...Or is it only I and Barnabas who must work for a living? Who serves as a soldier at his own expense? Who plants a vineyard and does not eat of its grapes? Who tends a flock and does not drink of the milk? ... For it is written in the Law of Moses: "Do not muzzle an ox while it is treading out the grain." Is it about the oxen that God is concerned? Surely He says this for us, doesn't he? Yes, this was written for us, because when the plowman plows and the thresher threshes, they ought to do so in the hopes of sharing in the harvest. If we have sown spiritual seed among you, is it too much if we reap a material harvest from you? If others have this right of support from you, shouldn't we have it all the more? – 1 Corinthians 9:4, 5a, 6-7, & 9 -12 (NIV)

The next fundraiser was for a new home mission work in the area. John decided the theme would be "I Want That Mountain." John challenged the church by dividing the church in half. One half was Jacob and the other half Caleb. The side that raised the most money would serve the other side a meal.

The challenge was on. The ladies of this church, known for their cooking, had lots of dinners to raise the funds. I can't remember which side won, but I do remember the missionary coming to the church. He had grown up in the area, so he knew their beliefs in giving. He thought he was going to get $300 at the most. This six-foot plus man sat on the front row, with his arms spread out on either side of him, legs straight out in front of him.

We had put the Caleb chart on one poster board and Jacob on another poster. That day we had put them together and, on the back, we had made it look like a check. When John turned the poster around to show the amount collected. The amount sent to his mission account was over $3,000. The missionary almost slid off the pew and hit the floor.

To Be Or Not To Be

Age will count against a pastor in one way or another. Either he's too young or too old. There is a small window where his age doesn't matter. Right after we were married, a man at the church we attended told me Jesus would have done better if He had been older when He started His ministry! I couldn't believe what I was hearing.

Steve and Fern started attending our church and they asked John for advice during a fellowship dinner. Steve looked at John and said, "You know there are certain ages that think they know everything - 13, 16, 21, and 26."

John sat there nodding his head yes. Steve proceeded to ask John how to get his teenage step-son's attention. John sat quietly listening to the couple and then informed them how to do it. They were to get the boy to sit at a dining table with the wall behind him. Then push the table to the wall at one end so the boy wouldn't have a way out until he listened to his parents.

Steve and Fern thanked John for the advice. I could see the people in the fellowship hall were ready to burst out laughing because they knew John was only 26. Going gray early doesn't always hurt. Just for information, according to the couple, the advice worked.

Dressed For Work

John had grown up back east and was trained, by pastors. They taught him how to dress, how to preach to various groups of people, visit hospitals, etc. These days the way a pastor dresses is completely different. But 27 years ago, pastors still dressed up every day.

John went out to visit in his suit. The farmer who John went to visit looked at him, laughed, and said John had to work with him if John wanted to visit. John came home and said he had to wear work clothes when going to visit. From then on, John had bib overhauls. He even wore them to visit at the hospitals. Funny thing was the people loved him for doing so. This told them he wasn't looking down on them; he was one of them.

I Needed A Job

> *In the same way, the Lord has commanded that those who preach the gospel should receive their living from the gospel." - 1 Corinthians 9:14 (NIV)*

My husband doesn't demand his salary when taking a church. This means things can be very tough for us, especially when outside income isn't available.

Now this church paid somewhat better than the last. We were up to $150 - $200 a week. Not much to live on with student loans, car payments, and such.

The church bragged around town how little they paid the pastor. At one point, we were living on only

$10 a week. That included purchasing gas for our car.

I applied for jobs all over town. I went to the bank, but they sent me to a mining company. I went there, and because of my previous job, they knew I knew they were operating illegally. Before I got home from leaving my application, they had called John and said I wasn't getting hired. Walmart wouldn't hire me. You can be so overqualified you can't get work. That was my case.

I babysat a little boy in the parsonage until he started school. Nick would say he came to see John instead of my taking care of him. John was his favorite person in the world.

Cinnamon Rolls

At this church, they had a yearly revival. Their custom was having the pastor and his wife take care of the evangelist. That I understood, but they brought food to the parsonage to feed the evangelist and the pastor.

I had grown up with families taking turns having the evangelist and the pastor over for meals during the revival. This way the church members would have the ability to become acquainted with the evangelist.

After several years, you pretty much knew who was sending what to the house. This time one lady, who had never previously participated, sent her husband with cinnamon rolls.

I made spaghetti to go along with the leftovers for lunch that day. John and the evangelist were fighting over the last of Karen's fresh strawberry pie.

I am highly allergic to strawberries, so I decided I'd eat a cinnamon roll. There was a twang, but I thought it was the spaghetti sauce and the cinnamon in the roll. It was Mother's Day weekend and the evangelist was going to Ft. Smith on Friday night after the service to have time with his wife and son. I thought it would be nice if I sent breakfast with him. So, I made my overnight coffee cake. I placed half of the coffee cake and half of the cinnamon rolls in a foil pan and gave the pan to Mark as he was leaving.

The next morning, I asked John if he would like a cinnamon roll with his coffee. He was thrilled at the thought of having a cinnamon roll. We both had the shock of our lives with the first bite. Colleen had poured vinegar over the cinnamon rolls after they were baked! I was horrified. All I could think of was that I had sent half a pan of these cinnamon rolls as a blessing.

That evening after the service, I apologized to Mark. He told me that he thought I was pulling a practical joke. Mark and John had been crazy all week. One-night John and Mark were jumping off the front porch in rapture practice, to see who jumped highest.

Even though he had eaten supper before getting on the road for the hour-long drive, he got hungry. It was dark when Mark left our house, so he couldn't see what was in the foil pan. He just knew I had given him goodies and he stuck his hand into the foil pan and pulled out the first thing his hand landed on, A CINNAMON ROLL. He took one bite and threw the whole pan out the window.

We didn't say anything to the other members, nor did we humiliate Colleen by questioning the vinegar.

Not long after this, we had our monthly community singing and fellowship. Colleen's cinnamon rolls were on the counter. Mabel was diabetic and watched what she ate. Her son-in-law Jesse, whom John was trying to lead to the Lord, was supposed to be there that night. Jesse hadn't shown up. Mabel made a show of getting a takeout plate for Jesse. "I'll take Jesse some of this fried chicken, some of this . . . and, oh, nobody has taken any of Colleen's cinnamon rolls." All heads quickly turned towards her. If she could have read minds, I know she would've heard "NOOOO!!!" I thought for sure every person would have whip lash. It turns out the vinegar over the cinnamon rolls was normal with Colleen. To this day I haven't learned why. The only thing I did learn was she didn't do it as a way to hurt us.

Praying The Boat Sinks

I urge, then, first of all, that petitions, prayers, intercession and thanksgiving be made for all people— for kings and all those in authority, that we may live peaceful and quiet lives in all godliness and holiness. This is good, and pleases God our Savior, who wants all people to be saved and to come to a knowledge of the truth. For there is one God and one mediator between God and mankind, the man Christ Jesus, who gave himself as a ransom for all people. This has now been witnessed to at the proper time. – 1 Timothy 2:1-6 (NIV)

Duke only worked from January 1 through April. You've got it, an accountant. The rest of the time he was on the lake fishing. He told us he couldn't be at church as he worked so hard all the time. Sunday was his time to relax.

Duke's wife was an invalid. Jean wanted to be in church as much as she could. In order for this to happen, several of us took turns driving her and their two children to church.

As time went by John became more and more upset with this man's attitude towards church and his family. When taking prayer requests, John asked everyone to pray Duke's boat would sink.

The news of the pastor's prayer got to Duke, and he started coming to church.

Praying They Vomit

There was a man in our church who was busy looking for people to introduce to the Lord. He asked John to visit two Vietnam vets who were alcoholics. Not only were they drunk, but they smoked like chimneys. John is very allergic to cigarette smoke. They wouldn't listen to him, so John started praying that these two men would vomit every time they drank.

The Lord honored John's prayer. Walter informed the men why they were getting sick. One man cursed John. Sometime later he died, never accepting the Good News of Jesus Christ. The second man accepted the Lord and became sober. He came to church and played with the little kids as they walked by him. After about a month he cut his hair and wanted to be baptized. Two weeks after his baptism, he died in his sleep.

Are You Listening?

Occasionally while preaching, John has said the wrong person with the Biblical account. I will never forget *Moses* coming off the ark! The congregation yells "Amen" but I'm sitting there saying *Moses*?!

Another faux pas happened after someone sang a song. He said that song brought tears to his ears. After church, a lady walked up to him and checked his ears for tears.

Judged

Do your best to present yourself to God as one approved, a worker who does not need to be ashamed and who correctly handles the word of truth. – 2 Timothy 2:15 (NIV)

One little lady informed John he had to be lazy as his hands were soft. John told her he was sorry she felt that way. As a pastor, he was to spend time in prayer and preparing himself for preaching God's Word.

Comparing Us To God?

But Jesus often withdrew to lonely places and prayed. – Luke 5:16 (NIV)

This same lady approached us and informed us that God doesn't go on vacation, so, neither should we. John explained to her that Jesus had to get away sometimes.

Mother's Day Call

Trust in the Lord with all your heart
and lean not on your own
understanding.- Proverbs 3:5 (NIV)

When God calls, you never know what He has planned for you. When the Lord told John he needed to return to college, we were filled with excitement and dread.

Here we are, living on $10 a week after bills are paid; how are we moving, getting a job and a place to live? But God can and does come through.

Never could I guess how the Lord would come through on the move to Nashville. With no jobs, how were we going to get there, and pay for classes? We prayed and trusted the Lord would answer.

Sunday afternoons are nap time. We woke to the phone ringing. John answered and my brother, Scott, wished him a happy Mother's Day. John in turn did the same to Scott. Scott asked about our move. Could he move us? Yes, of course.

The day came and Scott, his wife, mother-in-law, and my nieces helped us load the U-Haul. They were moving machines.

College, Here We Come?

Trusting the Lord was calling us to Nashville we went without employment. The Lord had an apartment for us on campus. The Lord supplied John with a job working for another Christian college.

After unpacking for a couple weeks, I heard a knock on the door. When I got there nobody was there, only a post-it note. It was from the treasurer of the college asking if I wanted a job. If so, come to his office in the morning for an interview. I was hired part-time working in the Business Office. Within a month of my employment I was working full-time. GOD IS GOOD!

When we left for college, John's intention was to sit out of the ministry until he finished college. We moved in late July, but by September, John wasn't a happy camper. As we sat in worship services, his leg danced so hard that everyone on the pew felt the movement. He wasn't listening to the sermon, he was writing out sermons.

The Bible College Christian Service director contacted John. A non-denominational church had called wanting a pastor. Would John be interested? John desperately wanted to preach.

We went out Sunday morning. It was 45 minutes outside Nashville. We were out in the middle of nowhere. We walked in to find a congregation of about 13 people. The previous pastor had resigned to care for his wife. John was voted in that very day. This began six wonderful years.

God Comes Through

If anything, unplanned is going to happen, it will happen to my husband. The church had a storage building next to the church. On the morning of our first homecoming, the men headed to the building to pull out all the extra tables and chairs. John followed them to the building, and as they opened the door, a wasp flew out and stung John between the eyes. John, being highly allergic to wasp stings, immediately got sick.

One of the men rushed to the nearest community to get Benadryl for John. All he could find was a small bottle of children's strength. John drank the whole bottle of Benadryl. John had turned totally white and mainly sat staring straight ahead. A young man who was attending the church and felt the Lord had called him to preach, asked John if he wanted him to preach. John said no.

The service went on like it should to the point of preaching. John was still as white as a sheet. He got up, went to the pulpit, and started preaching. His color came back. He preached clearly. As soon as he finished, he was white as a sheet once again. Never underestimate what the Lord can do.

But ye are a chosen generation, a royal priesthood, an holy nation, a peculiar people; that ye should shew forth the praises of him who hath called you out of darkness into his marvelous light – 1 Peter 2:9 (KJV)

Hand Of God

I was asked to sing "It's Beginning to Rain" at a homecoming service. The song is about God pouring His Spirit out like rain, but when I sing it, physical rain happens most of the time.

Lunch was on the church grounds. We walked out of the church to have lunch and you could see dark rain clouds all around. The sun was shining down on the church and the area around the church. The kids of the church kept looking at the sky waiting for everyone to be drenched. After the meal, the church had a group come sing. As everyone was settling in their pews, the rain came down hard. It let up in time for the day's services to end.

God used this as a lesson to the kids that God loved that we were worshipping Him.

Concussion

When John accepted one church, they only met on Sunday mornings. They had been accustomed to having a circuit preacher for years. They were just glad to have a preacher once a week. With prayer and the Lord convicting them, we started having Sunday evening services at our home for a while.

After a year, we finally made it to three services per week. During this time the Lord sent a woman who had been raised Catholic to our church. Deborah came to every service.

John was teaching on Wednesday evenings about the persecution of the church. We loaned *Foxes Book of Martyrs* to families of the church. They were in turn, passing the book around. To our horror we found one of the ladies had loaned the book to Deborah.

If you haven't read the book, a lot of the persecution came from the Catholic Church. Suddenly, Deborah wasn't attending church. She'd never missed a service before this.

Jesus is "'the stone you builders rejected, which has become the cornerstone.' Salvation is found in no one else, for there is no other name under heaven given to mankind by which we must be saved." – Acts 4:11-12 (NIV)

One Monday night, John was putting together our new entertainment center when the phone rang. It was Deborah and she wanted to talk with John. She had gone out of town for seminars. While she was gone, the Lord had convicted her. On the busy highways around DC, she pulled over and accepted the Lord as her Savior. Not only that, she wanted to be baptized Wednesday night. John was so excited about the news that he gave himself a concussion on the entertainment center. A retired missionary doctor at the college thought John had no business baptizing on Wednesday. There was no way my husband was not baptizing her that night!

Ferret

Many of you may be acquainted with the song by Ray Stevens, *The Mississippi Squirrel Revival* aka *The Squirrel Went Berserk.*

My husband wasn't blessed to hear the song until we moved the Nashville. Within months of hearing it for the first time, the song took on a whole new meaning for him.

My husband had taken a couple, who weren't fitting in at college, under his wing. They were backward. John convinced them to come to our church. Everything was fine; the people accepted them.

As they drove the 30 to 45 minutes to the church, they might stop and pick up a turtle or two, which, after church, they would proudly display.

You, Lord, preserve both people and animals. – Psalm 36:6b (NIV)

The church decided to have a revival. John asked Pat, the man who had led him to the Lord, if Pat would preach. Pat was wearing a silk suit that morning. This couple came into the church with their little boys as usual, but today they evidently thought it was bring your ferret to church day.

The wife had the furry creature in her hands and upon approaching Pat, threw it to him to catch. Fortunately, Pat caught it before its claws could ruin his suit.

John asked them to take it to their car. They refused saying they had its cage, which they brought into the church. Before I go further, I want to remind you this was a small country church. On each side of the stage in the sanctuary were rooms which were closed off by wooden accordion doors. The kitchen was behind there.

The husband put the ferret in the cage and placed it in the opposite room from the youth's Sunday school class. The adults met for Sunday school in the sanctuary. With the partitions closed you could hear the ferret on its wheel squeaking a merry tune, which was music only to him.

Then the fearful thing happened, just before Sunday school was over, the wheel stopped! Then Southern Belles were screaming in the sanctuary. "Pastor, get that thing out of here or we'll never come back!"

John had to force the couple to remove the creature from the church. The poor couple couldn't understand why nobody wanted it in church.

After the service, we went to a restaurant for lunch. As we sat there, John informed me he never wanted to hear the Mississippi Squirrel song again. He had lived it and didn't want to be reminded of it.

Crushes On The Pastor

Ministers can become objects of desire because of the gentleness and understanding they exhibit, and because they take time to listen. Many men are unaware, blind, or thrilled at the attention. As a wife, we are the buffer that keeps them out of possible trouble.

John is so blind to flirting. Our church had a monthly singing on Saturday nights along with a time of food fellowship. The church would ask a group to come sing as well as having anyone in the community who wanted to sing. One of the favorite groups was a female group. Each of them was married, but their husbands never came. I happened to notice the lead singer touching John a lot. After it had happened on a couple of Saturday nights, I brought it to John's attention. The next time the group came, John noticed the minute her hand went onto his back. He moved away from her.

Moreover, the LORD said, "Because the daughters of Zion are proud and walk with heads held high and seductive eyes, and go along with mincing steps and tinkle the bangles on their feet, therefore the Lord will afflict the scalp of the daughters of Zion with scabs, and the LORD will make their foreheads bare." – Isaiah 3:16-17 (NASV)

At another church, before we moved there, a young woman had divorced her husband because of abuse. She had a little girl no more than one-and-a-half years old. The little girl would get loose from her mother go and stand by John as he was preaching. Sometimes she stood on her head. The mother didn't chase her as it would have only made more noise than she already made. John never acknowledged the child beside him. After the service was over he would pick up the child and carry her to the back to her mother. I noticed the look in the young woman's eyes. John crushed her as he preached on Valentine's Sunday that he praised God for giving me to him. She never came to church again!

Oh, Christmas Tree

I don't know if you have Christmas trees in your church during the Christmas season or not. In one church they used real trees for several years. A dear sweet man who lived next door was given the task of cutting down a tree.

This man didn't have a lot of common sense. He cut the tree down and brought it into the church shortly after cutting it down. Upon entering church, we found mice had ridden in with the tree. Most of the mice drowned in the toilets while looking for water. That's not what you want to see when entering the restroom.

The following year, we didn't have mice, but this time the tree had been marked by deer. Walking into the church and smelling deer urine in the air is also not something you want! The tree was removed and someone donated what we call the "toilet brush fake tree." The name says it all!

The Lord took care of that ugly tree the following fall. The church was being used for a Christian music video. The film crew arrived before John got there to unlock the door. When they arrived, they surprised thieves who had broken into the church's shed. They had stolen the tree and decorations. The film crew tried to film the thieves getting away. As the thieves left, some of the decorations fell in the middle of the road.

A member of our church who owned a production company, took care of providing us with a Christmas tree from then on. Her idea of a beautiful tree was 100 lights per foot of tree! It was stunning!

Family For Those Away From Home

We were never given children, but God has blessed us at times with teens and young adults. When we lived in larger communities we had the ability to be family to those who were away from home. College students have been the main ones that have found our home as their home away from home. This has truly blessed us. Many Sundays they came home from church and ate with us.

Line Dancing, Playing Instruments

While attending a Christian college, the students are to participate in Christian service. This could be Big Brothers/Big Sisters, a local mission, or working in a local church. John was pastoring but John has had them teach Sunday school, lead singing, or play the piano or organ.

At one church, we had two girls coming who fit in very well. One played the piano and the other the organ. They had John and me laughing so many times. The college was very stern on dancing. At one of the church functions, a young woman who had a dance studio came. Line dancing was popular at the time, so the girls learned how to line dance and were taking it back to the dorm to teach other girls.

At one point my mother-in-law was attending church after moving to our area. John's mother was very set in her ways. She thought you were to marry the first person you dated. That was the only person who was to speak to you. One Sunday, two of the politest young men came to the church and spoke to each person. Because these young men had said "Good Morning" to John's niece, she was called a whore by John's mother. She got mad and informed his niece so. Everyone heard what she said. She then threw a tantrum. After the service was over, we were having a fellowship dinner. Lizzie, being barely five-foot-tall told me if I needed her to take John's mom down outside, she'd do it. Unfortunately, I was tempted.

If the girls were having a bad weekend, on Sunday morning they would ask me to lead the church in singing the most unredeemable song in a hymnal: "If Men Go to Hell, Who Cares!" I never allowed it.

Another Ministry

As I stated, when we moved to Nashville, John was going to college. He started working for another Bible college; but when the need came for another night watchman, he applied. This began a new ministry as well. John, while working night watch and later in cleaning, ministered to students and witnessed to the neighbors around the college.

Go West

The church was growing, and things were going well, but God put on our hearts it was time to leave. We had gone to visit my parents, and while there, we went out to the western part of the state. John hadn't been west of Wichita, Kansas, and he felt the Lord drawing him to Kansas.

This would be a new world for him; I was going home in a sense.

Quirks

All Scripture is God-breathed and is useful for teaching, rebuking, correcting and training in righteousness, so that the servant of God may be thoroughly equipped for every good work. – 2 Timothy 3:16-17 (NIV)

My husband doesn't stand still while preaching. During the first pastorate, John would come home after church wondering why he was so tired. I informed him everyone at church had been given good neck exercises. The congregation felt like they were at a tennis match. He would move from one side of the church to the other.

With people having hearing problems, a microphone was put at the pulpit. This worked for a short time. Then a ham radio operator started interfering during the sermon, and foul language would come through the sound system.

With everyone horrified, they changed to a corded microphone which John clipped to his tie. John became the entertainment. Everyone would get tickled. John had a set path he took around the pulpit. Just as a dog gets wound around a post, John did the same with the pulpit. He would get wrapped around the pulpit and then have to unwind. We also found that John had worn the carpet down around the pulpit.

Doing weddings made John really nervous. I told him not to lock his legs as that could make him fall over in the ceremony. What does he do? He **rocks heel to toe** all through the ceremony! In one wedding, the groomsmen followed suit. I was just glad nobody was recording the ceremony. Praise the Lord; he no longer does the rocking.

On Call 24/7

As a pastor he is on call 24/7. You can't tell your husband that work ends at a certain time of the day. This also means his days off may not be days off.

We had a member who suffered from PTSD. He would have nightmares of abuse, especially during storms. He would call in the middle of the night. I would answer the phone and wake John up, so he could help the man. I would lay there and pray as John would talk him out of reliving the abuse. After John was successful, he would hang up and go back to sleep, and I'd lay there wide awake.

Another time, it was a man who was drunk in a hotel. He had found the Gideon Bible in the room and started reading it. I have no idea of how he got the number to call us, other than God Himself. But he called John, and John talked to him for hours. This was early Sunday, around one or two in the morning. That morning, the man came to church and gave his heart to the Lord.

Tracts And The Police

Not all communities welcome outreach. John went out with invitations to our church and was placing them on doors only to have the police come tell him it was against the law. I have feared his arrest more than once concerning this.

Out Of The Blue

One Sunday afternoon, we received a call from Dr. Meyer, an English professor at the Bible College John had attended, and where I had worked. The church he was attending needed a pastor. He asked if we would consider moving back to Nashville.

Arrangements had been made for us to stay in an apartment on the Bible College campus. We were to call the night watchman and he would let us in since we would be arriving very late at night. I contacted the night watchman when we were about two miles outside of Nashville. I had no idea who this guy was, and he didn't know who I was, other than the campus guest using the apartment.

When we pulled up to the apartment building, John stepped out of the car and a figure wearing a parka in April came towards us. The young man, upon seeing John, broke out in a huge grin, ran to John, and hugged him. It was Kenny, a young man from the Caribbean. John knew that smile coming towards him. John had been the one who had hired Kenny six years earlier.

The next day John was to meet with Dr. Meyer, and I was informed I had a meeting with the college as well. The college wanted me back in the position I had left, but with benefits, as if I had never left.

One of my favorite unloads came after we had driven the moving truck across four states. We had loaded the truck and couldn't sleep after the house was empty. We got in the truck, and we drove all night and most of the next day.

Upon arriving, my husband was dead on his feet. We were met by one of the church's teens. He made a call and within an hour the men from the church showed up. By this time, my husband was asleep in a corner. The men unloaded the truck and even set up the bed while John slept.

CHAPTER 6

DEATH & FUNERALS

Precious in the sight of the LORD is the death of his faithful servants. - Psalm 116:15 (NIV)

Death And Dying

As much as John prefers funerals over weddings, they are very hard on him. The second funeral John officiated after we were married was for our piano player at church. Grace was a dear lady who kept Joe, her husband of over 76 years, in check. Joe was known to upset people. John never knew his grandma, and Grace took John on as another one of her kids.

Until we moved there, John had never had bologna salad. Every time Grace made some, a container came to our house for John.

There are so many aspects of the ministry that we just take for granted until you must deal with them. When we got married, I knew funerals would be a part of the ministry. But once you are close to the church family, it becomes harder. We get to watch new life come into the world which is a blessing. I never really thought about my part in the passing of a saint until it happened. Oh, I had lost grandparents, cousins, been to funerals, but I was not there when the passing took place.

The first time I faced death with a church member, it was with Grace. She and Joe had never spent a night away from each other until the night before the Lord called her home.

As the surgeon prepared to do a heart catheterization on Grace, she had a heart attack and was in a coma when we got there. We were shocked, since we only knew she was going to have tests done. Living an hour away from the hospital made for a stressful drive.

The hospital had a little room used for observation and located off the individual ICU room. It was for observing. We stood there as her grandkids pleaded with her? While they pleaded with her, I watched Grace's heart rate remain very low. John told me I couldn't cry in front of Grace. If I was going to have a problem, then, I wasn't to go in. I stood quietly watching as my husband read scripture to her. Every time John read to Grace, her heart rate increased. I begged John over and over to just keep reading. Before dawn, as we sat in the waiting area, Jesus took her home.

John and a former pastor of this church performed the funeral. This other pastor focused on his own wife's death. John stood in the pulpit and cried and cried over losing this wonderful woman. The family told John after the service how much it meant to them that he loved her like they did.

It wasn't long until we experienced death again. It was Sunday morning, and we were at church. We found out an elderly church member with Alzheimer's was at the hospital and not expected to live. The whole church left for the hospital. Upon arriving, we were told she wanted the pastor's wife. I hadn't known her when her mind was clear. She didn't know me. As I stood there she begged me to help her. All I could do was hold her hand and pray. I prayed and prayed. She wouldn't let go of my hand. Finally, my husband had to come get me, so her daughter could see her mom. As we left the room, she went home to the Lord.

We went into the waiting area where everyone was told the news. Everyone paired up and cried on each other's shoulders. I felt alone as my husband and the attending doctor cried on each other's shoulders.

During the second pastorate, my husband preformed 36 funerals in three years. I attended more than that as I would sing with a group from church almost every other week.

While working on our taxes, my brother teased John when he saw how many funerals John had done in one year. Scott asked John if he was preaching heaven so well that people were dying to get in.

Other times when we've been called to the hospital, I've grabbed snacks and activities to keep little ones occupied while adults are with the family member. Yes, I become a babysitter. Many times, this is the first time they have contact with the church.

I wish I could say the Lord has given me wonderful words to say to the family, but I never feel adequate.

Sometimes death is long and drawn out. Yes, like in cases of cancer. As draining as it is for the family, know it is that way for your husband and you. Trying to encourage the family, praying, and keeping long hours not only physically drains you, but can also affect you spiritually.

Even when you are totally beat, you'll find that you are to jump in to help the next family.

Hallelujah Handshake

John was called to perform a funeral of a woman who had once attended our church but had become a shut-in before we came. John had been out to visit her several times and she wanted her pastor to do the service.

John was asked to come by the house before the funeral to see the family. I rode with him to the house. For your information, Oklahoma isn't necessarily flat. We were going down a steep hill outside of town on the way to the house. John looked over at me and said, "Pray. We don't have any brakes." I prayed and prayed. God was good as the house was at the bottom of the hill, off the highway. We slowed down to a stop in front of the house.

After visiting with the family, John got back into the car. He asked me to give him my hand. He then dropped what he pulled out of his suit pocket into my hand. "What is it?" There was a $100 bill! Never had John received money for a funeral until then. With that $100, we were able to fix the car, get a vacuum cleaner, and buy groceries.

Oh, a hallelujah handshake is when money is in the hand of one person and they place it in your hand, unseen by others, while you are shaking hands.

Police Escort

Most of the time, funerals are as follows: someone passes away, you visit the family to console them, and then you have the services.

There can be funerals where you feel like you are in a Hollywood movie.

These funerals come out of left field. You just can't help but sit there with your mouth hanging open. At one such funeral, the sister of the deceased called John, requesting he officiate the service. John didn't know either of the women. This woman felt like John was her pastor as she and I both sold Avon! The deceased was visiting her when she passed away. She wanted John to do the service. John will never turn down doing a funeral, as it is a chance to witness to the family. The sons of the deceased didn't want a funeral or even a coffin. They just wanted their mother dumped in a ditch.

The aunt kept calling about how her nephews were acting. John told her to get a restraining order. He gave her the sheriff's name and number. John had to help her do it. All of this took place on Friday. Come Sunday evening, we get a call that the nephews were at her house and drunk.

Would she call the sheriff? No, she calls my husband. She wants John to call the sheriff! John finally does so, but since the sheriff was so aggravated, he told John he had to meet him there. John went. After arriving, John, the sheriff, and the aunt were talking when, out of the corner of my husband's eye, he saw one of the nephews raise a beer bottle to hit the sheriff over the head. Before John knew it, he had decked the guy. Yes!!! The sheriff informed John if we weren't leaving the community he would hire John as a deputy.

When John arrived home, first he told me I wasn't attending the funeral; then he told me the details of all that happened. Again, I was told not to let anyone know he had decked someone. I looked at him and laughed. The sheriff was related to and lived next door to one of our church members. You know he had to brag on John's quick actions.

John had already informed our church family, who wanted to attend and take food to the funeral, that he would take the food. Little did he know at the time, this funeral would need to have a police escort.

The Sheep

Just as people are destined to die once, and after that to face judgment, so Christ was sacrificed once to take away the sins of many; and he will appear a second time, not to bear sin, but to bring salvation to those who are waiting for him. – Hebrews 9:27-28 (NIV)

On the news one evening we saw that a man had been murdered by a friend after leaving a Christmas party. The next day we received a call from a former member who happened to be a distant cousin of the deceased. The family didn't have a minister, so he had offered John. John said he'd do it even though it was taking place on Christmas Eve.

The family wouldn't meet with us until the morning of the funeral. We were informed the deceased was a devout Christian. John asked what his favorite scripture was.

"The one with the sheep."

John sat there wondering what they were talking about.

I asked, "The Lord Is My Shepherd?"

"That's IT!!"

As we began working on the service order, the family informed us the deceased had recorded a song expressing his love for Christ and they wanted it played. It was decided it would be the first song played.

When we arrived at the funeral home chapel, there were lots of gangster rappers. There was a service across the hall for the cousin of the deceased, who was also murdered somewhere else on the same night. These people couldn't sit long enough to go through the service. People were leaving to go out to smoke and/or drink.

John wanted me to stay in the hall while he did the service he was asked to do. I told him he needed someone in there praying for him while he did the funeral service. I sat on the back row, surrounded by guys who had chains hanging from the waistband of their jeans to their knees, or longer, and their boxers were showing above their jeans.

Normally, one couple from church attended all the funerals associated with the church and their young son always attended with them. During this funeral, I was praising the Lord they hadn't come. Their son was open to learning new things and this funeral would have supplied him with more material than his parents would have liked.

My head, which was bowed in prayer when the song came on, immediately popped up. "*#@*, *#@*". I waited to see my husband's reaction. He stunned me. Instead of walking out, which was what I expected, he quietly got up and preached that the deceased had made his decision about where he wanted to be, and he was there. He then told the congregation they also had a choice of where they wanted to be.

Normally John rides to the cemetery with the body, but this day he didn't. We sat in the car for 30 or 40 minutes waiting to go to the cemetery. Once at the cemetery, John told me to stay in the car. It was bitter cold, snow was falling; and the tent at the gravesite was full of cigarette smoke. After the graveside service was over, the funeral home director told John the reason why it took so long to leave for the cemetery. The funeral home employee who had driven the hearse carrying the cousin had gotten out of the vehicle to open the gate at the family's private cemetery. While he was opening the gate, a friend of the deceased hijacked the hearse, so the deceased could have one last joy ride. Needless to say, this was a day we and those working at the funeral home will not forget!

The funeral home employees apologized for not listening to the song prior to the service. They also informed John there had been discussion of asking John to do both funerals.

A Suicide

The saddest funeral we ever did was for a woman in our church who committed suicide. It was late in the afternoon on a Wednesday. The little boy I babysat hadn't been picked up, so he would probably go with us to church and be picked up from there.

John got a call from the police saying he was needed at the scene. I called the boy's mom and informed her she needed to come and get her son immediately. She flew over to get him. I rode with John to Suzanne's home. She and her son lived together. We knew she had financial problems from time to time; but, she hadn't said anything to anyone the last time she was at church. There was only a graveside service. Her body was in a pine box. Our church felt we had let her down. While I was at the grocery store weeks later, I was told she had been in. She told them that her finances were bad and that she thought she'd go home and kill herself. Nobody alerted us or the authorities.

Visiting The Sick And Hurting

Visiting hospitals, nursing homes, and mental health facilities was another thing I never thought about being a part of my life in the ministry. I have been blessed by not being a patient in a hospital since cutting teeth as an infant. Also, at the time I was growing up, kids weren't allowed to visit people in the hospital. So, upon entering a hospital to visit, I have this irrational fear the staff will notice some unseen stamp which indicates my time is up and I must be checked in.

My fear came as a teenager. I belonged to an organization for girls through my school. One of the things we did was community service - visiting the nursing homes. Most of the visits were at Christmas to sing to the patients, normally in a living area.

Then our sponsor/teacher decided we should take turns visiting the nursing home in pairs. Praise the Lord that nursing homes aren't as dark, depressing, and as smelly as they were then. During one of the visits I made, I entered a very dark room as the lady called to me from the darkness. Once in the room, she grabbed my hand and asked who I was. I told her, and she asked if my dad was Kenneth Sallee. When I told her he was, she then held tighter to my hand and wouldn't let go. It turned out my dad had, on more than one occasion, visited the nursing home with other men from church. This woman loved my dad. Unfortunately for me the darkness, smell, and her grip petrified me.

John and I are a team. Most generally I go visit with him. I can even go into a hospital or nursing home by myself now.

In one community, the Minister Alliance took turns on Sundays with services at the nursing home and this community also had a mental health facility. I was uneasy when we got there, but not as much as our church members. John, though, walked right in as if walking into any other building and I followed. On the other hand, our church family clung to the walls as if the center of the hallway was filled with something disgusting or there was a huge hole in the floor.

I must say I was very impressed with my husband. The patients came up to him and surrounded him. I watched as they patted both of us. When they wanted a hug, he hugged them. Some of the patients noticed my wedding band and told me I was married. I informed them I was, to John. As we stood singing hymns, John and those with him lined up and swayed to the song. Our people were still plastered to the wall and missed a blessing.

From that time on, when we drove by this facility the patients who were outside would yell, "Hi, Brother John."

As a pastor's wife, my territory was broadened. I was taken out of my comfort zone.

We who are strong have an obligation to bear with the failings of the weak, and not to please ourselves. – Romans 15:1 (ESV)

CHAPTER 7

WEDDINGS

Husbands, love your wives, just as Christ loved the church and gave himself up for her to make her holy, cleansing her by the washing with water through the word, and to present her to himself as a radiant church, without stain or wrinkle or any other blemish, but holy and blameless. In this same way, husbands ought to love their wives as their own bodies. He who loves his wife loves himself. After all, no one ever hated their own body, but they feed and care for their body, just as Christ does the church— for we are members of his body. "For this reason a man will leave his father and mother and be united to his wife, and the two will become one flesh." This is a profound mystery—but I am talking about Christ and the church. However, each one of you also must love his wife as he loves himself, and the wife must respect her husband. – Ephesians 5:25-33 (NIV)

Up front, I have to say John prefers doing funerals over weddings. As he puts it, only God will bring the deceased out of the ground. As much as couples tell you they will love each other until death, they are in love with the idea of being in love.

They view weddings as fun parties, but they are so much more. They are contracts between the couple and the Lord. As much as people might want to leave Him out, He is in the middle of the contract. He made the institution of marriage. Another thing many people are not aware of is that your attendance at a wedding is a contract between you and the couple. You are saying you will do everything you can to help this marriage work.

Shortly after moving to one community, we were asked to come to a wedding associated with the church. Our church members were upset John hadn't been asked to perform the ceremony. Once the ceremony began, John was thrilled he wasn't asked. Everyone did a do-si-do down the aisle! Yes, even the minister did. That's not happening with this pastor.

Then the mayor's daughter wanted to get married at Grandma's church. Again, John wasn't asked to perform the marriage. We sat at the back of the church with a couple from our church. It came time for the bride to come down the aisle. She entered by herself. Her dad had refused to be a part of the marriage. When John saw this, he informed me he wouldn't have performed the ceremony as there were problems from the get-go. Until things were resolved, and the father could walk her down the aisle, he wouldn't have done the wedding. John told me the marriage wasn't going to last. Three months later, the bride was living with another man.

Green Dress

While pastoring a little country church, we found out it was popular for weddings as it was rustic, in a valley, and there was a bed and breakfast just down the road where they could have their reception, if they liked. The bed and breakfast would have a horse-drawn carriage take the bride and groom to the reception. It was a Cinderella ending to the ceremony.

One wedding couple wanted to be married in the church and asked John to perform the wedding. Now this church was in a remote little area. You could get lost trying to find it. The bride and groom's directions to the church had the wedding party lost. The groom informed us that he had written a song to the bride and his music teacher was coming to play it. She would be a large woman wearing a green dress. We waited as long as we could. I closed the back doors after having the bride and her father go down the aisle. Then suddenly, standing beside me was a young man barely five-foot-tall, weighing 90 pounds at the most and wearing a green suit. He informed me he was there to play for the groom.

Now came the tricky part, the chamber musicians had taken the piano benches. We went in a side door and searched. They had missed an old a rickety bench, which he grabbed, I threw open the partition door by the piano just in time for the song to be sung. Wedding saved.

Icing

Before I go much further into wedding memories I need to make a statement. Brides, DO NOT freak out when something goes wrong the day of the wedding, especially before the ceremony. That makes for smooth sailing later on. It clears the tension.

At ours, my little cousin either ate something that upset her stomach, or the excitement of the wedding, or it could've been both, but the poor girl vomited in the vestibule about 30 minutes before I went down the aisle with my dad. My dad quickly found a mop and cleaned it up. My dad saved the day.

The reason I wanted to tell you this is that the next wedding is an example of a disaster to the bride and future sister-in-law.

The sister of the groom made the wedding cake. The woman put the cake together before heading to the church. Just a tip - do NOT have a cake put together to travel a distance, especially on country or bumpy roads. My mom made wedding cakes as gifts to couples. We went from Kansas to Chicago with separate layers of cakes with crumb coating only and had to check every so often to make sure the cake hadn't cracked or fallen apart. You can guess how this went. The cake did not fare well in the trunk on the country roads. Upon arriving at the church, about a fourth of the cake had lost all the icing. When the bride got to the church, her eyes landed on the icing covering the ground. The bride was in tears thinking her wedding was destroyed.

The groom's sister got in her vehicle and headed to the nearest town to buy a cake. I encouraged the bride to use the original cake, just have the damaged side at the back. I'm glad to say the bride and groom did so. In doing so, the crushed sister-in-law was encouraged.

You've Got To Be Kidding

John was contacted about performing a wedding at our church. As soon as he said a requirement for him to perform the wedding was six sessions of marriage counseling, he was no longer administering the vows. This wedding was the day before our last Sunday at the church as we were moving away. The lady in charge of events at the church had another member attend the wedding to make sure the church was left in good shape. The church was having a reception for us the next day and she needed to know how much work would need to be done to have it ready.

Sunday morning the lady who had been at the ceremony told John why they didn't want John doing the service. She gave a detailed account of the church and the wedding.

It started out with bagpipes playing in the parking lot and chamber music in the sanctuary. The bride was escorted down the aisle by her two ex-husbands, who also gave her away!

Since our lady was so interested in all of this, she decided to visit with the men at the reception. Upon doing so, she found out that after the honeymoon, ALL OF THEM WOULD BE LIVING TOGETHER.

A Line In The Sand

John was asked to do his niece's wedding. Due to the family being upset about the wedding, John declined. We decided to attend the wedding. That day the Lord gave John laryngitis. Yes, John couldn't speak, and it was good thing.

I ducked in to see the bride 15 minutes before the time to start. Everything was fine. I went into the sanctuary and sat down with John and other church members. The time came for the ceremony to begin and nothing happened.

It turned out John's niece, the groom, and the maid of honor went back to Nashville to do her makeup after I had spoken to them. This was a 30-minute drive from the church. We sat for over an hour waiting for the bride and groom to get back.

As we sat there, John got angrier and angrier. Our church people were upset as it was Christmas time and they could be out doing their Christmas shopping.

John's niece and the groom came in laughing at what they had done. Praise the Lord, the minister doing the ceremony rebuked them. If her uncle had done the service, the church would have been empty when they returned.

Put In Her Place

I was hired as a nanny for a couple who owned the Co-Op. Their family was the richest in the community. His sister, Nancy, and Grandma attended our church.

Nancy was getting married at our church. At the time of the rehearsal, there was no bride, bride's mom, or grandma. After an hour of waiting, in came Nancy, her mother, and grandma. By now the groom, who was upset sitting in the church all this time, says so everyone could hear, "Where have you been? We've been here an hour!"

Nancy burst into tears. John grabbed her and took her to his office. People were still upset about the hour and now this. After 10 minutes passed, John returned to the sanctuary. I was informed I needed to sit with the bride.

When I got to the room, Nancy told me why they were

late. They were getting ready to come to the rehearsal when her mother decided that Nancy needed to do her hair and nails as well as grandma's. You did what mama wanted no matter what.

While I sat with Nancy, John was laying the wedding party low; informing them they were not to hinder the bride but help her. When I found out what John said, I thought for sure I was losing my job. The next day at the reception, Nancy's father walked up to us and told John he had never in his life been so proud of a man as when John put his wife in her place.

Cleavage

My husband was taught by a pastor to never look at a woman below her shoulders, so you won't get in trouble and accused of lusting.

We never see the wedding party's attire until the wedding. At this wedding the groomsmen were dressed in 1880's coats and vests. Very striking!

John wore a black choir robe, so he wouldn't have to worry about standing out like a sore thumb in wedding photos. Plus, we couldn't afford to rent clothing to match the various weddings.

Then there was the bride. She had her dress cut to her navel! I watched as my husband performed the vows looking over the heads of the wedding party. It was rather funny to watch.

CHAPTER 8

KIDS

Jesus said, "Let the little children come to me, and do not hinder them, for the kingdom of heaven belongs to such as these." – Matthew 19:14 (NIV)

One little boy kept us in stitches. Tommy's parents didn't participate in Halloween so getting candy from trick-or-treating was out of his reach. Our church had a cookout and hayride. Everyone brought their leftover candy.

The candy was left inside the church. My parents were visiting, and my dad came outside laughing. Tommy was wearing a lined jean jacket. He had made a hole in a pocket and was stuffing candy bars in the lining. He had even bent the candy bars to fit around his body. Once his parents found out what he was doing, they had him empty his jacket.

Tommy was probably seven at the time and had about 30 candy bars in that little jacket. His parents were horrified as we sat laughing. It wasn't that his parents didn't allow him to have candy. He just figured he'd get as much as he could while he had the chance.

Christmas programs are challenging for those directing. I had that year's program narrated so lines didn't need to be memorized. This didn't mean the cast shouldn't listen to when to enter the stage, and other directions.

Tommy decided I needed an assistant that morning. He stood there telling the teenagers when to go out and then it was his turn. He was one of the wise men. As the main character in the story, I had borrowed a turban from the college to make him a true wise man. I had hung a sash down from the turban. Oh, how Tommy loved it. He got into a dream state rubbing his hands on the sash, so much so the narrator had to improvise on the script. You've got to love him!

I praise God for kids who really get into the program and want to make it even better. We had one Christmas program where a boy was to play an old man driving up in a truck. My idea was to have him come up the aisle with a steering wheel in his hands. Not Larry! He came Sunday morning with a refrigerator box made into a truck and before coming down the aisle, he poured baby powder on his head to make himself have white hair. Little touches make things special.

Faithful

Kids can have such tender hearts. We had three little brothers who would hop on the city bus to come to church. In the winter, they waited for the bus without coats or gloves.

We picked up a group of kids at one home on Sunday mornings. We knew every Sunday there would be at least one junior high girl riding with us. Hopefully, we would get her older sister to come. Her little brother preferred the church that had video games instead of lessons like our Sunday school and Children's Church. One morning when I picked her up, she shared her nightmare with me. She dreamed she missed church; if only adults would see this as a nightmare!

Toy Barbie Jeep

Not everyone has wisdom as to how to entertain their little ones in church. There was a man who brought his granddaughter with him to church - just her, his Bible, and himself. Since we didn't have a nursery, everybody at church helped keep her quiet.

When grandma came with her husband to church, she brought toys that would disturb the service. One Sunday, she brought a Barbie jeep. The church had hardwood floors under the pews and carpet in the aisles.

That same day a young man who was straight out of the military special services came to church. During the preaching, when Satan really wants to work, the little girl took the jeep and gave it a good roll. Everyone heard the tires clacking on the hardwood floor. It went to the front of the church and across the aisle, hitting the young man in the ankle. He looked down, and back up to listen to the sermon, unamused.

Boxers

...for all have sinned and fall short of the glory of God. – Romans 3:23 (NIV)

Why young men think that showing their underwear is impressive, I'll never know. The former pastor's grandson started coming to our church exposing his boxers. The elderly southern belles were horrified at this. They complained to John over and over. John talked to the boy's father, but nothing changed because he saw nothing wrong and laughed it off.

Then one Sunday, as John was standing at the back of the church, Hunter started to walk by. To my horror, John informed Hunter that if he was going to show everyone his boxers, he might as well show all of his boxers. John then grabbed Hunter's jeans and yanked them to his knees! From that point on, when he got to church, he adjusted his droopy pants so his boxers didn't show.

Stunned

You must teach what is in accord with sound doctrine. - Titus 2:1 (NIV)

Shortly after moving to our first pastorate, I was asked to teach the teens since the previous pastor's wife had been their teacher. No problem, I was used to teaching kids at church.

Before long, the topic of sex before marriage came up in the Sunday school lesson. The kids sat there like deer in head lights. There were a few questions but not many. Not surprising, right?

To date how long John and I have been married, a book titled "88 Reasons Christ is Coming Back in 88" had been released. The day predicted Jesus was coming back was a Sunday afternoon. Remember, we will not know the day or time when Christ is returning.

We had been invited that day to an older couple's house for lunch. We were relaxing after a great meal when we got a panic call from one of my girls, Sally. She was at the church and NEEDED TO GET RIGHT BEFORE CHRIST CAME THAT AFTERNOON. She was going straight to hell.

But about that day or hour no one knows, not even the angels in heaven, nor the Son, but only the Father. Be on guard! Be Alert! You do not know when that time will come. – Mark 13: 32-33 (NIV)

John and I rushed to the church where we found Sally sobbing at the altar.

John and I counseled her. As we did so, she opened up and told us that the pervious pastor's wife hadn't told them what God thought about sex before marriage. In fact, she had handed out birth control products to her class.

Sally's fear of going to hell had her in agony. After talking and praying, Sally was on the Lord's path.

Sit With An Adult

Have confidence in your leaders and submit to their authority, because they keep watch over you as those who must give an account. Do this so that their work will be a joy, not a burden, for that would be of no benefit to you. – Hebrews 13:17 (NIV)

Ninety-eight percent of the kids attending our church were bus kids. As with all kids during worship service, they wanted to sit with each other. Before the preaching portion of the service would begin, John gave the kids instructions. If you are caught talking during the service, he would stop the service and have them sit with an adult. Many times, John didn't even need to tell the kids to move. An adult near them would tell them they had to sit with an adult. To tell the truth, sometimes I think he needs to separate some of the adults!

One Sunday, John didn't even notice Missy and Amy were sitting on the front row talking. The pianist caught the two talking while John was preaching. Virginia whispered to them go sit with an adult. Missy was to sit with me and Amy was to go to her mom.

Amy made it just fine as she went to her mom. But, Missy had a problem, because I sat across the aisle. Doesn't sound too hard, right? But as I've said before, John loves walking while preaching. This day, John had zoned out everything going on around him. Every time Missy tried to come across the aisle, John stepped in Missy's way. This went on about four times before she finally got across the aisle. John wasn't even aware of what was going on. It was a snicker time for everyone except for John and Missy.

To Pie...Or Not To Pie

Unlike church attendance when I was growing up; now, 90% or more of kids come without their parents. Some of these kids have the worst home lives imaginable. We've tried our best to let these kids know they are loved. John has tried to let the kids know he is just a man, not someone on a pedestal. When the church had an Easter egg hunt, there was a contest where the ones who found the most eggs in each age group got to put a pie of whipped cream in a foil pan in John's face.

Each time the laughter was something. The desire to find the most eggs was even greater. One time a little girl refused to put the pie in John's face. Her Aunt Beth, 10 years old than her, did it for her. After Beth joyfully pied him, the little niece cupped John's face in her little hands with the saddest face. John laughed and told her it was okay. The next year, she creamed him.

Up, Up, And Away

As I have said, I was a nanny on a large ranch. We asked my employer if we could bring the kids from church out to fly kites. We were allowed to do so. John and I had the kids help put the kites together; then John helped them get the kites into the air. Things were going well. Then Missy's kite got away. The wind came just right and grabbed the kite and away it went. Missy chased after the kite, bawling all the way. We called after her. She returned sobbing, "I'm sorry, I'm sorry."

John called out to all the kids, "Yell "bye" to the kite."

Missy didn't understand because, at home, she would've been grounded or worse.

Spit Balls

Not every kid who comes to church is there to worship the Lord; nor do they even care how they act while at church. We had a group of teenage boys coming to church. They behaved pretty much during Sunday school, but once they got in church they would sit in the back of the church and throw spit balls to the front of the church; probably seeing who got theirs the farthest.

This would happen while prayer was going on. I sat three rows from the front. In front of me were two elderly couples. I would feel the spit ball go past my ear and know it went past the couple in front of me and then past the other couple. I'm sorry but this really got under my skin. The father who brought the boys thought it was funny. This man was a pastor's son!

One Sunday as we drove to the church, I told John I would be talking to the boys in Sunday school. If they still did it, I would be going to the back of the church to sit during the sermon.

I informed them how disrespectful it was towards the people at church and most importantly to the Lord. The saying "in one ear and out the other" comes to mind. It seemed I made them more determined. More spit balls than normal were flying during the prayer.

Before John would preach, the little kids would sing a song. Once I was through leading them, I looked at John and said I was going to the back. I grabbed my purse and

Bible and sat on the last pew with them. The boys proceeded to either lay their heads on the pew in front of them or throw their head back and sleep.

After the service, I got the boys together and told them they now get to clean the whole sanctuary. They informed me they would only pick up the spit balls. I said, "No, any and all trash."

As they argued with me, a father of two young girls stepped up. This man, who wasn't a Christian, informed the boys they were going to listen to me and do as I said. Robert was a man who could scare you. He was furious at how the boys had acted at church and very upset that the father who brought them thought the whole thing was funny.

This was the last time any of the boys and the father came to church.

Ruthie

One little girl would bring a little friend with her to church. This other little girl was just as cute as she could be. She had a beautiful smile and was very friendly. One Sunday she came to church with bruises on her face. Everyone asked her what had happened to her. She told us that she had fallen off her tricycle, but everyone knew that was not the truth.

Finally, one Sunday, John got down on his knees and told Ruthie that God loves her and that everybody else at Church loved her as well. He also told her God loves her so much He didn't want anybody to hurt her, but if anybody did, she should tell us.

The next Sunday she came with more bruises on her face. By this time, we realized what caused the bruises. They came from handprints from someone holding her face and squeezing it. After a few Sundays, Ruthie finally told John what had happened. Her stepmother had been squeezing her face whenever she was mad at her. John started calling DHS to get help for Ruthie. And unfortunately, they did not want to do anything as it was getting close to the holidays.

During this time, Ruthie and Crystal both came over to eat lunch with us one Sunday afternoon. As I was cooking lunch, I looked out into the living room to see Ruthie sitting next to John. All of the sudden, John got up and started walking. I could tell that he was angry, but I wasn't able to find out why.

John and I had been trying to adopt through DHS, so John went to our instructors to talk to them. Within a very short time Ruthie had been removed from the home. Unfortunately, we were not able to see her from then on.

Bible Man

I had been explaining salvation to my Sunday school class when Aaron, a younger boy in my class informed me he wasn't ready to get saved. He wanted nothing to do with it.

As class was beginning one Easter Sunday, Aaron told me of the resurrection, looked at me, and asked when he could get saved. We did it right then. We went down the hall to where his dad was printing the bulletins and told him. Dad told mom to come visit my class. Mom burst into tears as Aaron had been dedicated to the Lord on Easter and his salvation came on Easter.

As a side note, the most wonderful part of this was his baptism. His grandparents were back from the mission field, so his grandpa was able to baptize him.

I truly believe children should memorize scripture

verses. These days you must reward the kids or they won't even try. Aaron wasn't allowed candy, but I could give him sugar-free gum. Aaron was learning the verses like a sponge. He would recite one verse after another and received a piece of gum for each verse. The older kids made fun of him. They called him "Bible Man." It crushed him. I wasn't to know it was happening, but his mother wanted me to help. I decided to teach him about Jesus being tempted in the wilderness. I asked Aaron if he knew what Jesus used every time He rebuked Satan. Aaron looked up at me and asked if Jesus had to learn memory verses. I grinned and he took it as a yes. I explained that you can only fight Satan off with scripture. The teens who made fun of him couldn't even remember the verse "Jesus wept" in order to get a reward from me. He was too young at that time to understand that Jesus' words to Satan became the scriptures we know today. Fortunately, from then on, he was proud of knowing the verses.

A side note: now, ten years later, Aaron made his second mission trip to South America this summer.

Blessed are you when people insult you, persecute you and falsely say all kinds of evil against you because of me. Rejoice and be glad, because great is your reward in heaven, for in the same way they persecuted the prophets who were before you. - Matthew 5:11-12 (NIV)

"Robin Doesn't Talk To Me That Way"

I absolutely detest having Sunday school teachers not show up for class. Being sick is one thing, but to go out of town and not let someone know they need anyone to fill in upsets John and me.

One such Sunday, Aaron didn't have a teacher. I was teaching older boys. The pastor was busy, so Aaron's mom went in to teach him. Aaron didn't want her teaching at all. I was across the hall with my door open. At one point he looked across the hall and yelled "Miss Robin doesn't talk to me that way." I had to laugh as his mom wasn't doing anything wrong and I did talk to him that way.

Helping Out Can Lead To War

I have always stepped in where I am needed. At one church I taught Sunday school to the junior high/high school aged boys. It was rather new to me to be the only woman in the class. The boys did not want to use Sunday school books because they said they didn't get anything out of them. I knew boys liked wars and such, so I decided that we would start with the book of Joshua. They loved it. In fact, one young man was reading ahead during the week and could be seen in church approaching adults asking them if they ever read what was in the Bible. He just loved everything he was learning. His mom informed me he was doing this outside of church as well.

I had one mentally challenged young man who loved the account of Ehud in Judges 3:15-27. Every Sunday when class started, he would pretend to draw his sword.

On Wednesday nights, as they studied Joshua and Judges, the younger boys' class made swords by decorating paint stir sticks. They also made shields with poster board.

Looking Deep

I was teaching little boys on Wednesday nights, but I didn't have literature and needed something new to stimulate them. John suggested I should show them Biblical principles in everyday situations.

I looked at him cross-eyed. "What?"

John's reply was, "Teach them you can apply Biblical principles to everyday situations."

So, I reviewed Disney's *Horton Hears a Who*. I saw two types of witnessing.

The first type of witness was Horton. He knew what he knew; he wasn't ashamed to say it; and he wouldn't be swayed by others.

The second type of witness was the mayor. He cared more about what happened to his image than to tell what he knew.

Before we started to watch the movie, I asked them to call out who would be considered a good witness and who wasn't. Needless to say, my class loved the movie.

But, goal achieved! They also learned how to look at situations differently. Aaron's parents borrowed the movie, so the family could watch it and Aaron could point out what he had learned.

Not In My God's House

Rarely have I been able to attend an adult Sunday school class. I normally end up teaching a class.

I was asked to teach the junior high and teens at one church, because the teacher wanted a break to attend an adult class. This class was different from any other. I was the only white person and a girl named Josie had a chip on her shoulder. She didn't want to be taught; she made it known every week.

It took lots of prayer for me to even go into the class. I cried on the way to church one morning telling John how I just wanted run away from the class. After letting it all out, I felt I couldn't let Josie win. I went to the class and taught. God helped me. I'm not saying it was easy, but it got easier.

The mother of another girl in the class asked to have her daughter's birthday party at the church. The only church members invited were Josie, my husband, and, of course, me. As the party was going on in the basement, we heard running and jumping in the sanctuary. I ran up the stairs to find my "problem child Josie" standing in the center aisle. At the top of her lungs she yelled, "Stop it! You will not act this way IN MY GOD'S HOUSE."

I stood on the staircase landing in awe. John came running up and I grabbed him. Out of my mouth and through tears, came, "She's got it."

Not only did the other kids stop out of fear, but her relationship with me changed. I'm not saying there weren't times Josie was trouble, but we both changed toward each other.

As Popular As Britney Spears

The Lord has given each of us a gift. Mine is to be a pied-piper. Over the years, kids have flocked to me.

One Sunday a woman came to church with her mother and three young children. She had been a battered wife, and the children had been victims by hearing and seeing the violence. Their trust was gone. I asked the kids if they would like to go with me to wee church. After coaxing them, they got comfortable. I loved teaching them as they were little sponges. I had placed pictures of Bible accounts around the room. Every time they walked into the classroom they would tell me what was going on in each picture.

Everyone got tickled in the sanctuary if I stood up to head for their class, the kids would begin jumping over adults' legs to get to me. Before leaving every Sunday, I would bend down and they would run into my arms for a hug.

Their great-uncle was attending church as well. He looked at me in surprise and told me that in all the years as their uncle he had never had a hug.

Upon visiting with the family in their home, John and I were told I was as popular as Britney Spears! That really dates me!

At other times, John has utilized the pied-piper while counseling. A young couple needed marriage counseling. Their son was very shy and clung to them. John knew that Brandon would interfere or distract them during the counseling session. I was to see if I could occupy him.

For the longest time, I sat there while Brandon roamed the room. Occasionally, he would go jabber to his parents. Then all of the sudden he brought me a Bible and opened it to the dictionary. There were a few drawings, which he started pointing to while standing beside my leg. Suddenly, he crawled up into my lap talking in his baby talk about every drawing he could find.

Mom and dad were sitting there poking each other and speaking with the movement of their heads, excited that Brandon had accepted me. After this first visit, when I entered the house, I'd be told, "Come here," and I would be led to where he wanted me to play.

Game Boy

If we claim to be without sin, we deceive ourselves and the truth is not in us. If we confess our sins, he is faithful and just and will forgive us our sins and purify us from all unrighteousness. If we claim we have not sinned, we make him out to be a liar and his word is not in us. – 1 John 1:8-10 (NIV)

One Sunday I walked into class to find Eric with his Game Boy. I quickly informed him that it was to be put away and he better not take it into the worship service with him. He promptly put it down.

When I walked into the worship service there was Eric showing it to the one college professor who hated technology. I thought this gentleman would remind him to put it away during church. As the service began, Eric moved to the front row! Temptation got to Eric as John was preaching. I don't really need to say it, but Eric started playing with his Game Boy. John saw this and came down from the stage area, took the toy, while still preaching. He put it on the pulpit, looked at Eric, said "See me after church," then continued preaching, never losing his place.

After the service, John gave Eric the Game Boy but told him never to bring it to church again. It took Eric almost a year before he came back to church. After he returned, he apologized to John and mowed the church yard and ours as his offering to the Lord until he and his mom couldn't afford the long drive hauling the lawn equipment.

CHAPTER 9

SALVATION

For God so loved the world that He gave His one and only Son, that whoever believes in Him shall not perish but have eternal life. For God did not send His Son into the world to condemn the world, but to save the world through Him. Whoever believes in Him is not condemned, but whoever does not believe stands condemned already because they have not believed in the name of God's one and only Son. – John 3:16-18 (NIV)

Christmas And Salvation

We didn't have enough kids to put together a Christmas program, so John asked a young boy about 10 years old to read the account out of the second chapter of Luke. After the Christmas carols had been sung on the evening of the program, it was Lee's time to read the scripture. Lee walked up to John and whispered that he couldn't read the scripture. Why had he waited until now to tell John he couldn't? John asked if he had a problem reading some of the words.

Lee told John he could read it just fine. "Then what is the problem?" John asked. Why couldn't he read it? Lee said he couldn't read it until he got saved. As you can guess John lead him right then and there. Then Lee read the scripture. This was great, right? NO!! The church was having a party after the service and the members were upset that this took time from their party.

When Can I Get Saved?

In small churches, you don't have the resources to have a Sunday school teacher for every age class. At one church, I had preschool through junior high. Trying to teach on all age levels is hard.

Kevin, who was about 10, was asking questions about salvation and baptism. Everyone was trying to help me and being no help at all. I found how little they really understood. Kevin asked the questions again. I told him to ask the pastor when we got into the sanctuary.

When we went into the worship service, he sat with his grandmother, not asking John a thing. His grandmother invited us to lunch at her home. On the way there, I told John the situation. John was ready. After lunch, Kevin and John played basketball, but again there were no questions for John.

It went this way for a couple months. Then one morning, Kevin was sitting next to me as the altar call was given. He looked up at me and asked when John was going to let him get saved. I remember smiling and saying, "Go talk to John right now." He got up and accepted the Lord.

But what does it say? "The word is near you; it is in your mouth and in your heart," that is, the message concerning faith that we proclaim: If you declare with your mouth, "Jesus is Lord," and believe in your heart that God raised Him from the dead, you will be saved. For it is with your heart that you believe and are justified, and it is with your mouth that you profess your faith and are saved. As Scripture says, "Anyone who believes in Him will never be put to shame." ...for, "Everyone who calls on the name of the Lord will be saved." - Romans 10:8-11 & 13 (NIV)

Sisters

I had two little sisters named, Hannah and Jennifer, in my class. I was teaching about what Jesus has done for us. They weren't interested and changed the subject more than once.

One Sunday in Children's Church, I was teaching about John the Baptist and his baptizing Jesus. The girls, who had no interest before all of the sudden asked about salvation. I explained, and they looked at me and said, "Let's pray." They did it!!

If anyone acknowledges that Jesus is the Son of God, God lives in them and they in God. - 1 John 4:15 (NIV)

Vernon

I will give you a new heart and put a new spirit in you; I will remove from you your heart of stone and give you a heart of flesh. - Ezekiel 36:26 (NIV)

I knew after taking a witnessing class how hard it was to talk with others about Christ. When we moved to this community, Hazel asked John to visit her husband, Vernon. How she ever married him, we have no idea. He hated people; he would rather spend all his time with his dog and sheep. Vernon would go off for months and never call Hazel.

The song *I'm Mean, I'm Mean, You Know What I mean* from the musical *Popeye,* comes to mind when I think of Vernon. His language was horrible.

My first encounter with Vernon was when he was in the hospital. John made me stay in the hallway because he knew when he entered the room, cursing would begin. Oh, how true! You could hear it down the hall, and I'm sure neighboring rooms heard it as well.

One afternoon, John went to check on Vernon after he got home from the hospital. Vernon stood inside his house watching John as he got out of the car. He thought it would be funny to sic his dog on John. As soon as the dog got close to John's leg, John's mind went to his youth. John grabbed the dog by the long hair on its neck and threw it over his shoulder. The dog took off running towards Vernon. Vernon just stood in his doorway, laughing and laughing.

John was so stunned at what he had done. As soon as he came in the door at the parsonage, he told me I wasn't to tell the church what he had done.

Vernon had told Hazel what he had done to "that preacher" and John's reaction. A very upset Hazel called John. Vernon was bragging about what he had done to the preacher. Being worried at what Vernon might do in the future, she asked John not to visit again without her being at home.

A year or two later, I came in the sanctuary after Sunday school, and there was a visitor sitting next to Hazel. I hadn't heard her talk about a brother, but that was who I thought he was. After church was over, John and I stood greeting everyone. After Hazel and this man had shaken our hands, I ask our song leader and his daughter who the man was. IT WAS VERNON!! He looked nothing like Vernon. His countenance was totally changed. John and I had seen him enough that we knew his stony face. God's word says He will change a heart of stone to flesh and I saw it! Another pastor had convinced Vernon to go to a revival at his church on Friday night. He had given his heart to the Lord.

That same Sunday, Harry, another man to whom John had been witnessing, was saved. This put John's resignation on hold. He had planned after the morning worship service to announce we would be leaving the church in a couple of months so that John could further his college education. After we had prayed, and a couple of weeks had gone by, John finally made the announcement. As we stood once again greeting everyone after the service, Vernon approached John. Looking sternly at John, he asked John if someone was making us leave, as he would take care of them, and we knew he could do it!

The church was in the habit of celebrating the birthdays of the month by going out to eat. Before we left for Nashville, we went to a fish place for the birthday celebrations. Normally we would go to a chicken place in town. The fish restaurant was packed; it was more than crowded. The chairs at the table behind you were touching your chair. Once you sat down, you weren't getting out for a bathroom trip.

For the first time, Vernon and Hazel came along that night. I had watched several years earlier at a funeral dinner as Vernon sat on a rock away from anyone because he couldn't stand people. This night, the Lord proved once again how much Vernon had changed. While sitting at an eight-foot table, there was a baby at the table behind us. The baby probably wasn't two years old. This child was looking over his mother's shoulder and started patting Vernon on the shoulder. Vernon turned to the child and started talking baby talk to the child. God is good!

Vernon and Harry became great workers for the Lord, not only in the church but the community as well.

Nevertheless, God's solid foundation
stands firm, sealed with this inscription:
"The Lord knows those who are His,"
and, "Everyone who confesses the name

of the Lord must turn away from wickedness." - 2 Timothy 2:19 (NIV)

David And Goliath

Occasionally John will preach a sermon focused at the level of the young kids. Children's Church would be in the sanctuary in place of the adult service. John borrowed my boss's Shaquille O'Neal tennis shoe to help the congregation understand how big Goliath's feet were. One young man climbed a ladder to demonstrate how tall Goliath was. Then John used a young teenage boy to fill in as David.

But, as much as the youngsters participated, when there was an altar call it was a Vietnam Vet rather than a child who came to the altar. He prayed that the Lord would help him defeat his Goliath; drinking and drugs.

But God demonstrates His own love for us in this: While we were still sinners, Christ died for us. – Romans 5:8 (NIV)

Three Little Pigs Sermon

After being married about 15 years, I got to hear John's sermon of the Three Little Pigs. Shortly after we were married, a father in the church told me he wanted to hear John's Three Little Pigs sermon. John had done it in Children's Church. This man's son had told him about the sermon, and the man was very impressed with what he had heard.

When I finally heard the sermon, John had everyone involved. Everyone yelling, "Not by the hair on my chinnychin-chin!" was the best. Part of the fun was having the people over 70 also yelling and laughing as they took part. When John gave the altar call, a young father came to the altar and asked the Lord to help keep the Wolf, cigarettes, from breaking down his house.

As Youth Pastor, John preached a sermon that got him in trouble with the adults. John told the youth that as God's creations, we aren't to call each other names because in doing so you are calling the Creator that name. The church we were working in had a couple who were mentally challenged. They were related to members of the church. Caleb rebuked his dad who was making fun of the couple. Upon questioning, Caleb told his dad Brother John had told them in Children's Church that by making fun of this couple, he was making fun of God. The pastor called us into his office and expressed how upset parents were about this. John wasn't to be disciplining the adults. Needless to say, that was the beginning of the end of that position at this church.

Holy Ground

God has used various sermons to speak to people in different ways. A young married couple, who were also young in their spiritual walk, were coming to church. One Sunday morning, John preached on Moses's encounter with the Lord at the burning bush.

The message of Holy Ground impressed the husband in such a way that from that moment on, after arriving at church and sitting in the pew, his shoes came off.

Baptism

Each church can have a different baptismal practice. Some churches have their baptismal in the church and others might have a river, a creek, or a pond they use for baptisms. As a kid, one baptism was in a horse trough. We've had indoor baptisteries in all but one church. The creek across the road was where we gathered.

We stopped traffic each time. I loved singing *Shall We Gather at the River* as we were gathering by the creek.

There were challenges to baptizing outside: the weather and traffic. This one baptism was challenging in several ways. Firstly, it was cold and spitting snow. Secondly, when he was baptizing one young boy and the boy was under the water, a large catfish swam just inches from the boy's head. Does John continue with the baptism or let go of the boy and catch the fish? Hmm… John did the right thing in continuing with the baptism.

The whole Judean countryside and all the people of Jerusalem went out to Him. Confessing their sins, they were baptized by Him in the Jordan River. - Mark 1:5 (NIV)

John, Big Fred, and another minister, Henry, started meeting on Saturday mornings around six or seven. They met at that time because Henry had a saw mill and needed to be at work later in the morning. Just the three of them met for prayer for about three months before, out of the blue, Big Fred threw his Bible down on the table and said, "Ok! I'll get baptized." The subject hadn't been addressed by the other two, but the Lord had been convicting him about it.

Big Fred was big! They walked across the road to the creek and it took both Henry and John to baptize him. After they had done the baptism, I received a call asking for clothing and towels. From that point on, John had a change of clothing and towels in his truck because the Lord began truly working. Their group grew. Hell's Angels were getting saved and wanted to be baptized immediately. One Saturday I was called to drive 45 minutes to join them so that they could have more people witness their baptism.

With every church since, John has longed to see the Lord work as He did in that little church; still, we pray.

CHAPTER 10

RENO'S

Rains Came Down And Floods Came Up

It seems like a life time ago, but while living in Nashville, it started raining one Friday and it continued on Saturday. Saturday night, I sat down at the computer to do some work while John watched the news. I looked over at the TV and saw a building floating down a highway as semi-trucks sat at a standstill on an overpass. I asked John if it was in Japan, since the news anchor had talked of mud slides there. John said it was out by the airport. Why nothing within me was screaming: "flood, Robin, flood," I'll never know!

The next morning, I had to get up before six to give a pain pill to our little dog who was crying. It was still pouring. I turned on the TV and the weatherman said we were in a flood. They said all church services needed to be cancelled. I woke John, and the calls went out.

We praised the Lord our house and the church were on higher ground, so we weren't flooded. Several of our church members were flooded. When the water was down to where we could travel, we went to the church. The shingles had blown off and the roof had leaked into the hallways and the sanctuary.

Since members were helping other members who had lost so much at their homes, John tackled the damage to the church. Mice had invaded the church!

With all the debris from the ceiling, we had no idea there were mice until I was teaching on a Wednesday night. I opened our class with prayer when one boy screamed he saw a mouse. As I calmed them down, a mouse ran down the hall. The boys were sitting on the sofas with their knees up under their chins. Someone had donated the sofas to the church for the Children's Church room. After church was over, I informed John of the situation.

John found that the mice had made their nests in the very sofas where the boys sat to escape the mice. Both sofas were thrown out, along with a roll of carpet the church had intended to put in the kitchen. After carrying them out of the church, John called to tell me how many mice ran out of the sofas and carpet while they were carrying them out. I'm not scared of mice, but I wouldn't have been able to cope with having them running on me. Ugh!

I don't know how most people feel, but as for my husband and me, nothing tells the Lord and community how you feel about your Lord better than how you care for His House. Whether it's just painting the church or more work is done, it helps people understand the importance of respecting God's House.

I've learned that whenever work is being done, my husband will be in the middle of it. Not all men will jump in to help. Sometimes the people want the work done, but they don't want or know how to help. They just want it done, and it should be done without any cost.

While the renovation was going on in one room, it was discovered there were asbestos tiles under the carpet. Legally, they had to be removed. It was going to be expensive. My husband sat on a dolly with a scrapper and removed each and every one of those tiles.

Walking Into Heaven

Remodeling a church can cause great stress and disagreement. Members who normally get along well can become ready to draw lines in the sand. The sanctuary needed to be repaired and updated after the storms lifted the shingles, flooded the sanctuary, and destroyed the ceiling.

During renovation, we were not able to meet in the sanctuary; we were meeting in the fellowship hall. There was not much room and tempers were flaring. The new carpet was taking quite a while to arrive. Then when it came, they hadn't ordered enough, so it would take another four to six weeks before it arrived. John made an executive decision: just leave it as its natural color. After the carpet was installed, there was still discussion about the changes. But the comment which caused everyone to sit back and enjoy the new look was from a young boy. He told me the new sanctuary, "looks like you are walking into heaven."

And I will make them and the places all around my hill a blessing, and I will send down the showers in their season; they shall be showers of blessing. – Ezekiel 34:26 (NIV)

Renovation Living

One church needed to renovate the parsonage before we could move in. The church blessed us by providing us a place to live while the renovation was done. The church put us up in a local hotel with efficiency apartments. We lived there almost three months.

Do nothing out of selfish ambition or vain conceit. Rather, in humility value others above yourselves, not looking to your own interests but each of you to the interests of the others. – Philippians 2:3-4 (NIV)

Lord Of The Flies And Skunks

Sometimes you have those visitors you wish never came and they stay longer than you like. We were at a church where a cat got into the church ceiling through a vent. Once inside the church ceiling, it died. Oh, the smell! We couldn't get into the ceiling to find the deceased. The deceased had mourners who showed up and who wouldn't leave: flies.

John put out bug killer every day for more than five days to remove the flies. As soon as he removed yesterday's mourners, new ones showed up. We aren't talking a few, but hundreds!

Another time, John went over to the church on a Saturday night around nine. He called me and said that if he didn't call me back in 15 minutes, I was to call the police. He wasn't alone in the church. I was in a panic but not about to go to the church. I waited as I was told.

About 10 minutes passed and I got a call. The noise was coming from the woman's restroom. When John entered the bathroom, he was met by a baby skunk. He backed out and went to the kitchen and found some potato chips. He left a trail of chips, which the skunk ate on its way out of the church.

Watch Where You Step

Another time we had the carpet pulled up and were waiting for the new carpet to arrive. The previous carpet layers had used so many nails and staples, which were now sticking up everywhere. The carpet layer was going to take care of this when he laid the new carpet. Unexpectedly, we had a member pass away. The family wanted the funeral at the church. In order for chairs to be brought in for the funeral, John spent two days crawling on the floor removing all the nails and staples.

Snakes

John got really sick and kept collapsing after coughing. This mainly happened at home. We went to various doctors to try to find out what wrong. One doctor told John that when he felt like it was going to happen, he should to get down on the floor, so he would not hurt himself when passing out.

One Sunday, before we got the diagnosis that his

vocal cord had collapsed, John preached the morning service. As he came to the close of his sermon he began to cough. The coughing only got worse as we visited with the members leaving through the main entrance. John leaned against the wall for support. Someone asked him if he would like a chair. "No." Then he blacked out and slide down the wall. I bent over him and gently slapped his face until he came around.

Bless the heart of one lady who asked if I wanted her to use her medical alert button to get an ambulance. I told her it was for her, not just anyone who had a problem.

John was too weak to walk home to the parsonage. The fastest way to the parsonage was out the side door in the sanctuary. As two men led John to the parsonage, an older man, Matt, opened the door. If John's passing out wasn't exciting enough, a long black snake came flying in the church door. Ladies screamed. Then Matt began dancing on the snake and he danced until the snake was dead.

Only after the snake was dead did the men get John home. In the meantime, John had a little plan he formulated: a prank. Seeing as John is from Kentucky, he wanted to put a wicker basket on the offertory table. No snake handling for me!!

CHAPTER 11

BLESSINGS

Now we ask you, brothers and sisters, to acknowledge those who work hard among you, who care for you in the Lord and who admonish you. 13 Hold them in the highest regard in love because of their work. Live in peace with each other. 14 And we urge you, brothers and sisters, warn those who are idle and disruptive, encourage the disheartened, help the weak, be patient with everyone. - 1 Thessalonians 5:12-14 (NIV)

You Are Loved

The people showed their love for us by inviting us to their homes for meals; taking time to know us; and making John's favorite foods, like fresh strawberry pie, bologna salad, cherry pie, and others.

John was known to hug as members came by at the end of the service. If people in the community couldn't remember John's name, he was known as the hugging preacher.

The people at church noticed John's suit coat was worn, and they sent him to the local clothing store where he was to get a suit coat, two shirts, and two pairs of dress pants.

"And why do you worry about clothes? See how the lilies of the field grow. They do not labor or spin. Yet I tell you that not even Solomon in all his splendor was dressed like one of these. If that is how God clothes the grass of the field, which is here today and tomorrow is thrown in the fire, will He not much more clothe you"- Matthew 6:28-30a (NIV)

Every year the ladies would go to a women's retreat and each year my way was paid for and I was given a new nightgown and housecoat to take with me.

We also had a beautician who took care of our hair as her service to the Lord.

Poundings

The church gave us poundings several times a year. If you don't know what a pounding is, the church members give canned goods to the pastor and his family. Sometimes we might even be given meat and dairy as well. This really helps cut down on your grocery bill. I've been given several five-pound bags of flour or sugar at a pounding. If I had enough room in the freezer, the extra went into the freezer. John was thrilled because Spam was a staple in every pounding at one church.

Tooth Fairy

We never know when or how we will receive a blessing. Of all things; I had a tooth break on my birthday. John had taken me to Ruby Tuesday's for my birthday. I ordered a burger and fries. As I bit down into my sandwich, I broke a tooth. No, there wasn't anything wrong with my meal; my tooth just broke in half.

It took weeks for me to get in to see the dentist as she was booked solid. When I finally got in, she informed me how much it was going to cost to not have a gaping hole when I smiled.

There was no way we could afford this procedure. We asked the church for prayer and told them what the dentist said.

After church, a man, who had been attending our church for a few months, asked me if I knew what he did for a living. All John and I knew was he ran his own business, but we didn't know what it was. It turned out he made teeth!

Gary went to a dentist friend he worked with and made arrangements for me to pay a lower rate on the dental work. Gary would make the partial and the dentist would put it in.

After a visit with this dentist we walked down a few doors to Gary's shop. He matched the coloring of my teeth to this artificial tooth that he was making for me. To this day you cannot tell which tooth is not my real tooth. The tooth and the work were a gift from Gary.

Perfect In Weakness

But He said to me, "My grace is sufficient for you, for my power is made perfect in weakness." Therefore I will boast all the more gladly about my weaknesses, so that Christ's power may rest on me. – 2 Corinthians 12:9 (NIV)

John watches how disabled people are treated by everyone when entering a church. Eddie was loved by everyone, including the bus kids. He was mentally challenged. We don't know if this would have been the case if he had been educated at an early age or not; but, at a very young age, he was the first resident placed at a new nursing home.

When it came time for John to start preaching, Eddie would pull out a pocket notepad and a pencil, which he either handed to me or another lady. We were only to write down the scripture reference. Why? After he got back to the nursing home, he went to those who could read and asked them to look up the scripture and read it to him. Then he would tell them what John had preached. This way Eddie fulfilled the Great Commission.

The area ministers took turns going to the nursing home on Sundays to preach. If no pastor showed up, Eddie would call John. John would grab his coat and go to the nursing home to preach.

So shall My word be that goes forth from My mouth; It shall not return to Me void, But it shall accomplish what I please, And it shall prosper in the thing for which I sent it. – Isaiah 55:11 (NKJV)

Determined

Fight the good fight of the faith. Take hold of the eternal life to which you were called when you made your good confession in the presence of many witnesses. - 1 Timothy 6:12 (NIV)

Over the years I've come to realize those with disabilities are more determined than those of us with two working legs. I've witnessed a man fall out of his wheelchair and crawl to the altar. Sometimes, people with two working legs won't even walk there because they might be ridiculed.

There was a man named Howard who blessed John by being willing to go door-to-door inviting people to church. Howard suffered the effects of polio. He had braces on his legs and weather changes caused him great pain. Did this stop Howard? No. With braces on his legs, he went down stairs backwards on visitation. He asked John to baptize him. The morning came, and Howard slid down the steps so he could be baptized. That's determination and strong faith.

Thank You

Thank you for taking the time to read a few of my memories as a pastor's wife. I hope and pray it has brought joy, laughter, and enlightenment. Years ago, Christian comedian, Mark Lowry, speaking of his favorite Bible verse, stated "'It came to pass'; it didn't come to stay" as his favorite verse. God stated 464 times "it came to pass." Praise God this is so true. What has made me cry in pain in many cases has since brought laughter.

Made in the USA
Coppell, TX
21 November 2019

11686541R10075